# Positively!

## *Learning to Manage Negative Emotions*

**Robert Kerr**
**illustrated by Steve Meyers**

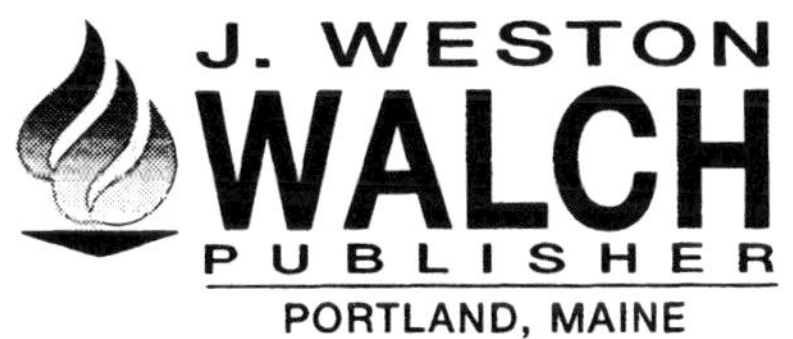

# User's Guide
# to
# *Walch Reproducible Books*

As part of our general effort to provide educational materials which are as practical and economical as possible, we have designated this publication a "reproducible book." The designation means that purchase of the book includes purchase of the right to limited reproduction of all pages on which this symbol appears:

Here is the basic Walch policy: We grant to individual purchasers of this book the right to make sufficient copies of reproducible pages for use by all students of a single teacher. This permission is limited to a single teacher, and does not apply to entire schools or school systems, so institutions purchasing the book should pass the permission on to a single teacher. Copying of the book or its parts for resale is prohibited.

Any questions regarding this policy or requests to purchase further reproduction rights should be addressed to:

Permissions Editor
J. Weston Walch, Publisher
321 Valley Street • P. O. Box 658
Portland, Maine 04104-0658

*Cover photography by CLEO Photography*

1 2 3 4 5 6 7 8 9 10

ISBN 0-8251-2869-2



Printed in the United States of America

## *Dedication*

*This program is about thinking—about what is rational, what is irrational—and it is written the hope that it may serve to tip the scales, even slightly for some in the direction of the former. I dedicate it to those two who were patient always with my own irrationalities: Dad and Mom; and to those two who now tolerate them: Heather and Jonathan.*

# Contents

# Foreword

## Positively! *in the 21st Century*

Most of the twentieth century was steeped in the authoritarianism of the Industrial Age. Young people getting ready for the industrial workforce, as I did, looked forward to one permanent job for the rest of their lives.

The industrial society had done much to foster sameness, predictability, order. Our credo for success was "learn to do what I am told." This was the way up the corporate ladder. Schools followed suit. My own schooling consisted of practicing rote skills, memorizing facts and formulae, doing without really questioning. This is not to be critical; Industrial Age schools did their job. They were preparing me for the autocratic, hierarchal, do-as-you-are-told workplace.

But times have changed. The Information Age is remarkably and refreshingly different from the previous age. It is quite likely that my own two children will never have "a job." They will probably do many things, and it is likely that they will change careers several times. They will need to be entrepreneurs. Young people entering the workforce, more and more, will be paid for their contribution, not their effort. The new marketplace wants no unthinking automatons; it wants confident self-starters, innovators, problem solvers, people who can work alone or in teams. It wants people who think for a living.

In the twenty-first century, being *confident,* being *socially effective,* is more important than ever. Discipline in our schools in now an issue of *empowerment,* of teaching young people a set of *inner controls.*

It is true, as Albert Ellis says, that almost all emotional disturbance is the result of negative, irrational thinking. *Positively!* teaches students the principles of Rational Self Instruction (RSI). RSI was developed from the conviction that children need more than behavior modification if they are to act in fair, responsible ways. To make behavior change more honest, more complete, children need to reexamine their own attitudes, to become more rational thinkers, to change their negative self-talk to positive self-talk.

Since *Positively! is* designed for use in the school setting, these 25 lessons deliberately focus on misbehavior related to the classroom, and specifically on the four goals of misbehavior outlined by the Adlerian psychologists: attention seeking, power seeking, revenge seeking, and assumed disability. But a reasonable expectation is that when a child begins to develop a more responsible approach to his behavior at school, he will generalize this behavior to other aspects of life.

Prior to its publication, RSI was tested in small group counseling sessions, in regular classrooms, and in special education classrooms. We found these things:

(1) Children enjoy the program. They become highly involved in the lessons, which provide opportunities for them to express themselves, to voice their thoughts, and sometimes to "ham it up" a little.

(2) After several lessons virtually all the children start to "get it." Getting it means they start to clue into the idea that we upset ourselves by what we tell ourselves.

(3) Children are helped by the program: some, a little; some, a fair amount; some, a lot.

(4) Teachers soon find that RSI becomes an important frame of reference with which to deal with problems and successes related to misbehavior. In the following set of lessons, students are introduced to a group of friends called the SAT pack. SAT is taken from the SAT plan, a four-step guide to Sensible Acting and Thinking. Kids in the SAT pack become the models by which to judge behavior in the classroom, on the playground, and even outside the school environment. Certain terminology—"overreaction," "appropriate reaction," "silly thinking," "sensible thinking," and so on— soon pervades the language used by students as they talk about their own behavior or someone else's.

*Positively! is* a program right for the twenty-first century. The 25 lessons serve as a sound program in emotional education for all children in school. All adults and children can learn to avoid excessive worry, low self-esteem, depression, and all forms of excessive behavior. As such, *Positively! is* used as a preventative and developmental program, and as part of the regular curriculum for all children.

We have to recognize that the misbehavior of some children will warrant a more immediate, intensive intervention. In a small group or one-to-one setting, RSI can be used in conjunction with the behavior management component to effect changes in children's attitudes and behavior. The Guidelines for Devising Student Contracts will help teachers to intervene in particular problems.

This is a program dedicated to the learners in our new age. It is critical today that all of our children learn how to develop sensible attitudes, how to think rationally about unfortunate events, how make successful plans. It is absolutely critical that children have success in managing their own negative emotions.

As a final note I wish to acknowledge the work of Albert Ellis, whose concepts formed much of the substance in *Positively!* I wish to thank Dr. Ellis for his personal encouragement and suggestions. Materials relating to his Rational Emotive Therapy are available from The Institute for Rational Emotive Therapy, 45 East 65th, New York, N.Y. 10021.

*—Rob Kerr*

# Introduction

## *Problems in Self-Control: Focusing on the Cognitive*

Ever since John Locke described the newborn infant's mind as a mere "blank slate," there have been those who would have us accept that we are all the absolute product of past conditioning. Indeed, "behavior mod" was the buzzword in schools even into the 1990's. To be sure, it has been difficult to argue with ardent behaviorists who have shown time after time that when reinforcers are consistently applied, they are able to change just about any undesired behavior.

The problem with strict behavior modification is not that it fails to work. Of course it works. The problem is that it hasn't worked for long. Researchers and teachers began to notice that the changed behavior often did not hold up well outside the engineered environment, nor did it hold up well over time. To add to these objections, some professionals simply did not like the cold mechanistic approach of behavior modification: it denied the child an active intellect and refused to acknowledge meaningful interventions other than a system of rewards and punishments.

For the past two decades a growing number of researchers have become interested in the role the child's "internal dialogue" plays in his behavior. In *Humanistic Psychotherapy,* Albert Ellis noted that even Ivan Pavlov stressed the relevance of cognitive factors—in what he called "the secondary signal system." Ellis maintained that "man is the kind of animal who becomes cognitively as well as reflexively conditioned" (p.195).

Aaron Beck's article in the first issue of *Behavior Therapy* has been credited with triggering the "cognitive revolution" in behavior therapy. The cognitive approach to therapy has since emerged as a philosophical alternative to the mechanistic approach of behaviorism, thus returning a measure of "freedom and dignity" to the individual.

A growing number of cognitive training programs have been developed for school children, most of them directed at deficits in self-control. Many of the programs have included a strong behavior management component with the cognitive training, hence the term *cognitive-behavioral training program.*

The promise of cognitive-behavioral programs has rested with their ability to produce generality and durability — the long-term effects that behavior modification programs were not showing. Though continued research is needed to improve these programs, the studies to date have given a great deal of credibility to the use of cognitive training. For example, in comparing the relative efficacy of medicine, behavior modification, and cognitive training as interventions with children having behavior problems, Keogh and Glover concluded that all were effective in different areas, but "cognitive training appeared to offer the greatest possibility of transfer or generalization."

Finally, the cognitive approach has added a warmer element to behaviorism: humanism. Educators of the twenty-first century will work with the *whole child*. Discipline, now, means empowerment. Children need to be taught how to manage their own emotions. The next generation of teachers and counselors will be lessening their grip on "behavior mod" and will be "going cognitive."

## *Rational Self-Instruction (RSI)*

Rational Self-Instruction (RSI) is a cognitive training program to help children (a) manage negative emotions more effectively through a process of rational thinking, and (b) behave more responsibly, particularly in the school. The program is particularly effective with children in grades 6 through 10.

RSI is a comprehensive educational program that includes:

25 lesson plans
student worksheets for each lesson
unit tests after each five-lesson unit
an optional behavioral component to solicit optimum cooperation and attention
a guide for devising student contracts for children with particular behavioral problems.

As such RSI may be used effectively by professionals in an educational setting:

by special education teachers with targeted groups such as

(a) contained special education classes
(b) withdrawal special education classes
(c) behavioral classes;

by counselors/psychologists/social workers

(d) with targeted groups in small group counseling sessions
(e) as a program for group guidance;

by regular classroom teachers

(f) with targeted groups within the class
(g) as a program for the whole class.

RSI was designed with three specific aims in mind:

(1) to incorporate useful suggestions from research on cognitive training;

(2) for students — to incorporate sound educational features;

(3) for teachers — to make the lessons concise, and easy to run.

As the name of the program suggests, rational self-instruction teaches children to talk to themselves in a sensible or rational way. The rationale is that

> Children misbehave from the desperate striving for self-worth.
>
> Poor self-worth is essentially a product of irrational/silly thinking — the negative, unproven, and destructive "self-talk" in which some children routinely engage during a particular event.
>
> Just as silly thinking and irresponsible behavior are learned, so are sensible thinking and responsible behavior.

The program is intended to show children that they upset themselves. The further purpose is to systematically teach children how to avoid upsetting themselves. As children learn to think sensibly about unfortunate events, they concurrently learn to act in fair, responsible ways.

## The Key Features of Rational Self-Instruction

In addition to teaching children to manage their own emotions through rational thinking and to behave more responsibly at school, RSI was built with three key features in mind. Each of the features is expressed here as a general aim:

(1) to help the children generalize what they learn in the lessons;

(2) to be comprehensive (a) effectively using features of cognitive-behavioral programs developed in research—specifically overt and covert self-instructions, modeling, and self-reinforcement; (b) employing the conceptual model of Rudolph Dreikurs for understanding misbehavior in the classroom; (c) employing the concept of "irrational belief systems" from Albert Ellis's Rational-Emotive Therapy; to have an educational format, resulting in practical easy-to-run lessons using sound principles of learning and motivation.

### *Generalizing What They Learn*

The popularity of cognitive training began with its power to make children apply what is learned to a variety of situations, and to have this hold up over a period of time. Donald Meichenbaum makes the important point that "generalization should be programmed rather than merely expected or lamented." Research has been helpful here, and RSI has followed several recommendations to help children generalize:

by teaching a general strategy that they can apply to a wide variety of situations
by actively involving the children in the program
by assigning homework activities whereby children apply concepts from the lessons
by telling the children to generalize.

## *A Comprehensive Program*

**Self-Instructions, Modeling, Self-Reinforcement.** For some time researchers have been developing and evaluating cognitive training procedures. Lamentably, these programs have been clinical and therefore not very suitable for classroom work.

RSI was designed as an educational program, incorporating the important features of various clinical programs. Self-instruction has been the essential feature in cognitive training, and RSI emphasizes the overt and covert self-instructions children may use to mediate their irrational thinking, and to guide them in appropriate behavior.

Modeling, an efficient teaching device in cognitive training, has been incorporated into RSI. Some of the lessons call for modeling on the part of the teacher, but more often the models in the lessons are the SAT Pack.

Self-reinforcement is another important feature of the program. In order to offset a dependency children are apt to acquire with an "external" system of rewards, RSI teaches children to reinforce their own performances. In the general strategy, called the SAT plan, children are taught to congratulate themselves for even attempting to act responsibly.

**Understanding Classroom Misbehavior.** The philosophy behind RSI supports the socio-teleologic theories of Adlerian psychology. The fundamental fact in human development is the dynamic and purposive striving of the psyche. A basic premise in Alfred Adler's thinking was that human action always has a definite purpose. Even if children do not always understand the intentions behind their own behavior, it is nevertheless important for us to understand that all children have their own private logic for acting the way they do.

Adler also emphasized that the child is a social being striving for a feeling of worth:

> Every departure from the social standard is an offense against right. This clash with objectivity makes itself felt first of all in the feeling of worthlessness.

In *Maintaining Sanity in the Classroom,* Dreikurs, Grunwald, and Pepper underline Adler's notions by admonishing teachers to understand misbehavior in terms of the child's social goal:

> As a social being, each child wants to belong. His behavior indicates the ways and means by which he tries to be significant. If the means are antisocial and disturbing, then the child did not develop the right idea about how to find his place.

Dreikurs et al. have presented a concise model, based on Adler's theories of human behavior, for understanding children's misbehavior in the classroom. According to their model, misbehavior occurs from one or several of four ways to attain self-worth:

(1) Attention seeking: to constantly manipulate the teacher's attention in a social situation. The private logic here is: "By manipulating your attention, I am worthwhile and important."

(2) Power seeking: to constantly oppose authority, to get into a power struggle with the teacher, to demonstrate power and control in a social situation. The private logic here is: "By showing you that I can do what I want, I am worthwhile and important."

(3) Revenge seeking: to constantly "get back" at the teacher, to hurt the teacher's feelings. The private logic here is: "By showing that I am able to hurt you, I prove that I am worthwhile and important."

(4) Assumed disability: to fail, to be left alone, to do nothing. The private logic here is: "I will punish you by punishing me, and then I have a measure of worth and importance."

RSI accepts the main premise that misbehavior occurs from a private sense of worthlessness, and the purpose of misbehaving is to gain back a sense of worth. These two ideas are central to the cognitive training in RSI. The lessons have also specifically addressed the four goals of misbehavior (conceptualized by Dreikurs et al.): attention seeking, power seeking, revenge seeking, and assumed disability.

**Irrational Beliefs.** Like Dreikurs, Dr. Albert Ellis believes that emotional disturbance is rooted in the desperate striving for self-worth. But more so than Dreikurs, the Rational-Emotive Therapy (RET) of Ellis focuses on irrational beliefs the child has about his own self-worth. In an educational setting, he uses his simple ABC model to show how we needlessly upset ourselves:

> Rational-emotive psychology holds that when an activating event occurs in a person's life at point A and is followed at point C by disturbed consequences (such as feelings of anxiety, hostility, depression, or inertia), A does not really cause C. Instead, C actually follows from B—the individual's belief system about what has happened to him at A. Thus, if a child fails at arithmetic at point A and is agitated and depressed at point C, it is not his failure that is causing these emotional consequences; rather it is his irrational belief at point C that he should not have failed; that it is awful for him to have done poorly; and that he is a worthless person for failing.

RSI embraces the central idea of RET: that feelings of self-worth are inextricably tied to one's thinking, "poor" self-worth being the product of an "irrational belief system." The lessons in RSI are sequential and teach children:

- to recognize "overreactions" (attention seeking, power seeking, revenge seeking, assumed disability);
- to realize that "overreactions" are caused by "silly beliefs";
- to challenge those silly beliefs;
- to change "silly beliefs" into "sensible beliefs."
- to create "calm, strong" action plans

In RSI Ellis's ABC model is employed as the HBR model:

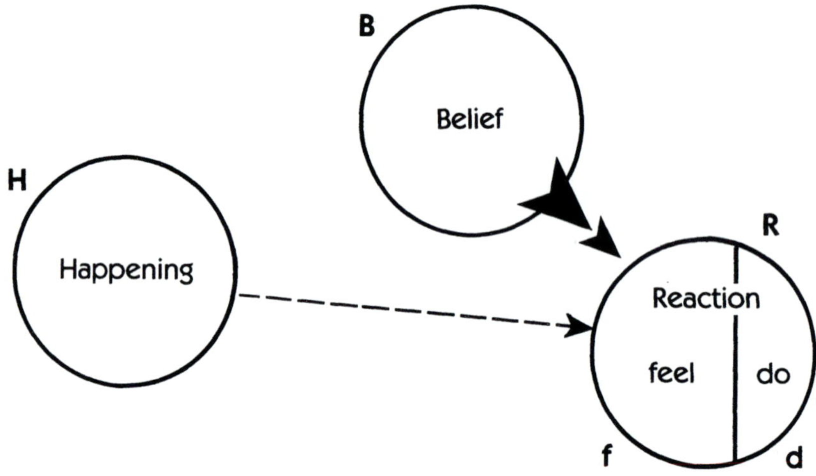


The "rational self-instruction" has children recognizing that overreactions at R (in terms of how I feel (f) and what I do (d)) are not really caused by the happening at H, but are caused by what I tell myself or believe at B. Such is the cognitive component in RSI.

The behavioral component in RSI makes use of a token reinforcement schedule. The system of "checks" is used to encourage children to both practice "sensible thinking" and behave more responsibly at school.

**The SAT Pack.** It is really the SAT Pack members who teach rational self-instruction to children. Whereas some children are presented as whining, self-castigating pessimists who typically overreact to a happening, the SAT Pack are shown to respond "appropriately" and "sensibly" to the same event. The fundamental difference — as RSI repeatedly shows — is what children tell themselves, what they believe.

**The SAT Plan.** The ultimate aim of the program is to get children to learn and spontaneously use the SAT plan. When they do this, they are practicing Rational Self-Instruction. The SAT plan is first introduced into the program in Lesson 16. It is a simple four-step scheme with a visual cue for each step. The students should be given praise and reinforcement for even attempting to use the SAT plan.

The first step is to have the child interrupt an overreaction by simply telling himself: "Stop. Relax."

The second step has the child thinking sensibly about what has happened. He has been practicing this in many previous lessons.

The third step prompts the child to come up with an alternative action to overreacting: a brief, sensible plan. A calm, assertive response is encouraged. The student reminds him or herself to "be calm, be strong."

The fourth cue reminds the child to self-reward, to say "Way to go!"

Clearly, RSI is a synthesis of the work and imagination of others, from the delivery format in other cognitive-behavioral programs to the theoretical stances of Adlerian psychology and RET.

## *Educational Features*

RSI was designed specifically for educators to be used in the school setting. Consequently, the program has a number of important educational features:

(a) Both the lesson plans and the student worksheets are clear, straightforward, and easy to follow.

(b) RSI is motivational. Students will enjoy the humor, high involvement, variety, and challenge in the lessons. The behavioral charts can be used to gain maximum participation and cooperation from "difficult" students.

(c) A mastery component is built into RSI. A criterion-based test follows each five-lesson unit. The tests will allow the instructor to evaluate each student's progress on an ongoing basis.

(d) RSI is a versatile program. Educators know their own needs best; the program should thus be tailored to meet the teacher's needs. A teacher may, for example, omit the behavior component of the program for larger regular or guidance classes, or the behavioral guidelines may be modified to achieve the best possible results.

(e) There is a good amount of experiential learning in RSI. The student worksheets and the activities—such as role-playing, small group work, imagery, student presentations, artwork and so on —serve to optimize motivation and involvement, and integrate the abstract concepts.

# Getting Started

The purpose of this section is to familiarize the instructor with the key elements of the program before starting. In addition, the instructor will have to reflect on certain questions presented here and make decisions about implementation.

**Are the Students Ready?** The students should have a familiarity with two activities presented in several of the lessons: role-playing and small group work. If they already have this familiarity, they are ready to start. If not, it may be a good idea to acquaint students with the two activities.

In role-playing the students should ideally see a responsibility in their roles as players and audience. The instructor should also stress the following:

(a) Role-playing is intended to be fun, but it also is intended to show something. As such, the exercise should always be taken seriously.

(b) The role of the audience is very important; the audience should be polite and never talk or in any way interrupt the skit.

(c) The dialogue is not rehearsed; there is only some brief planning time during which the actors should decide on their roles and quickly outline the skit.

Some students may be very shy in role-playing situations, others may be extremely silly. Take this as a matter of course. The rule of thumb is to accept what the children deliver, while trying to point out anything you can of a positive nature. Don't let the skit go on for too long; perhaps set a two-minute time limit.

In small-group activities students may need encouragement and direction in: becoming organized as a group; selecting a leader, spokesman, secretary, etc.; cooperating.

**Behavior Management.** In order to encourage cooperation during the lessons, completion of the homework, and application of the concepts in students' daily lives, a behavior component may be added to the program. You will need to read the section on the behavior component, then consider these questions:

Would your students benefit from a behavior modification component in the lessons?

Should the behavior component be modified in any way to suit your children's needs?

Would it be convenient to tie the "check" system to an ongoing classroom token system?

Do you want to involve the parents in the system?

Do you want to make use of the report card system?

You may utilize the behavior component fully, in part, or not at all. Since its purpose is to gain the cooperation and attention of each student, the decision will depend on both the makeup and the size of the group. With small groups and with "difficult" children, the behavior management system will definitely help the program. With large regular or guidance classes it may be difficult to chart the behavior of each student, and the full behavior program may be waived.

**Following the Lesson Plan.** The instructor should read over the lesson before it is taught. The lesson plans have been kept organized and concise so they can be referenced easily as you go through the lesson. The plan should be kept nearby during the lesson, as some activities require reading from it verbatim. Have the student worksheets ready to hand out. Each lesson plan follows the same format:

| | |
|---|---|
| Purpose: | a brief statement of the concept to be taught. |
| Review: | a brief activity to review a key concept from past lessons — usually the previous one. |
| Presentation: | the key concept is presented; often the student worksheets are used here. |
| Integration: | an activity in which students use the concept. |
| Recap: | reinforces the key concept of the lesson. This section is not always included. |
| Homework: | an assigned activity in which students apply the key concept. |

**Time.** Most lessons will take about 40 minutes, though this will depend on the size of the group. The suggestion is made to teach one or two lessons per week. The teacher will have to decide how to give absent students the missed instruction.

**Homework.** An "application" activity is assigned at the end of each lesson. Teachers should do these activities too: each will take very little preparation but should be a positive model for children to follow. Use of the "checks" in the Behavior Management Component may encourage students to complete the assignments; nevertheless, there are children who will probably resist or habitually neglect their homework. Don't make an issue out of this. Present your own homework, reinforce that of others and get on with the lesson in an encouraging fashion.

Make sure the students understand the assignment. The suggestion is made here that all children be supplied with homework booklet. In this booklet they may write down the assignment to refer to at home. They could also record the results of the assignment in this booklet. It is reasonable to insist that the students complete the homework in writing; this provides accountability in the exercise. Remember, though, that homework not done should not be dwelt upon!

The review section of each lesson allows time for the presentation of homework. If the group is large and time limits preclude each student presenting, have some present and briefly check others, or take up the homework at another time before the next lesson.

**Unit Tests.** At the end of each five-lesson unit there is a "criterion" or "unit" test. Testing may be done in a group as students write answers on paper. The teacher's job will be to clarify instructions and to help students understand the words.

A score for each question is given in the left margin. Answers are located on the page following each test. At the bottom of each unit test you will notice the "Criterion for Moving On." This is the minimum score to indicate satisfactory understanding of the concepts covered in the five previous lessons. The next unit should not be started until all students have reached this criterion.

For students not reaching the criterion on first testing, the teacher should plan to go over the key concepts. These tests should not be technically regarded as reliable and valid measures, but they will give a rough indication of whether or not the student has understood the material. The tests also create an incentive for children to attend to the lessons, and provide a review of the material.

**The Hot Seat.** In Lessons 17, 19, 21, and 23 some students are selected to work in the "Hot Seat" — which may simply be a chair at the front or center of the group. Here, the teacher presents the student with a potentially frustrating situation (read from the lesson plan). The situations involve attention seeking (Lesson 17), power seeking (19), revenge seeking (21), and giving up (23). The student in the Hot Seat is prompted to work through the situation in a fair and responsible manner, using the SAT plan.

The following situation, taken from Lesson 17, deals with attention-seeking behavior. The teacher reads this:

> Everyone is getting ready to write an exam. You hate exams, and you hate it when no one is paying attention to you. You tell yourself that you will feel better if everyone would laugh at you. You decide to lean back in your chair and "accidentally" fall backwards. But before you do, you think of the SAT plan. What do you tell yourself?

Here is an example of how the dialogue might proceed:

*Student*: Stop. Relax.
*Teacher*: Yes, good. Now, what's the second step?
*S*: Think sensibly.
*T*: So think sensibly about being ignored by everyone. What does it really mean if the class is ignoring you?
*S*: It certainly doesn't mean I am not important! And it won't make me any more important if everyone turns around and laughs at me for falling off my chair.
*T*: That's sensible enough. Now, go on to the third step.
*S*: I make a plan. I will be calm and strong. First, I will remind myself that I am important even if people ignore me sometimes. Second, I should be patient right now and wait until school is over to get together with my friends. Also, I should try to concentrate on the exam.
*T*: Excellent plan! What should you remember to do?
*S*: Congratulate myself.
*T*: So do it.
*S*: Hey, I finally acted fairly and responsibly. Way to go!

Some students, of course, will need more direction and prompting to work through the situation. The teacher should also accept prompts and suggestions from the group.

**Atmosphere.** On the one hand, firmness and consistency are to be expected; children should be as responsible here as in any other class. In addition fairness and consistency should be exercised in giving rewards.

On the other hand, it is important to have a salubrious climate in the classroom, with a focus on:

personal progress rather than competition
cooperation
a success orientation
encouragement

**Go Beyond the Lessons.** Remember that the ultimate aim of RSI is to have children applying the SAT plan to the normal frustrations of life. The lessons alone will probably not insure this aim; no program will. Perhaps the strongest suggestion to be made to the teacher is to use the program, the characters, the concepts whenever the opportunity arises.

Ask the children if they are practicing the SAT plan. Have class discussions about incidents that arise at school, using the SAT plan to point out ways to deal with them. The SAT Pack could be effective models in your counseling sessions with children, and in classroom discipline. The point is: children are more apt to apply and generalize their learning when the teacher goes beyond the lessons and stresses the concepts of rational thinking and behaving in everyday life.

# *The Behavioral Component*

In order to get the most cooperation and attention from each student, a schedule of token reinforcement can be used. As mentioned previously, the teacher will have to make a decision about whether to use the behavioral component of the program fully, in part, or not at all.

The full behavioral component would give children the opportunity to earn "checks" and subsequently exchange them for rewards or certificates. Conversely, a "response-cost" schedule has checks taken away in the event of uncooperative behavior.

**Homework Checks.** From Lessons 1 through 25 each student will be assigned homework. The homework requires that the student engage in a practical activity and write it down — in this way the student can be held more accountable. Presentation of homework is included as the first part of each new lesson, though teachers may wish to have this done the next day (this would certainly allow more time to complete each lesson).

The teacher should evaluate each child's homework presentation. This can be quickly and efficiently accomplished by marking the "Daily Checks" sheet.

3 checks: done very well
2 checks: done fairly well
1 check : done poorly
0 checks: not attempted at all

**Test Checks.** These are earned according to the number of times the child tries the test to reach the "criterion to move on."

3 checks: reached criterion on first testing
2 checks: reached criterion on second testing
1 check : reached criterion on third or subsequent testing

**Bonus Checks.** At the end of Lesson 16 students are informed of the opportunity to earn bonus checks. Bonus checks are added to the student's account if he reports using the SAT plan to avoid overreacting in real life. This reporting could be done immediately after the unit test or on one or two mornings each week. If the student can tell the class about using the SAT plan, he should be given credit for the checks. In addition, the student should be praised for such attempts, or encouraged to try to earn the checks next time. This is, indeed, an "honor system" and the teacher shouldn't be overly concerned about verifying reports.

**Response Cost.** Each child will have one check taken away on the Daily Check Sheet if he is extremely uncooperative during that lesson.

Minor infractions should not result in the response cost, although the teacher may warn the student that further disruptions will result in the loss of a check. No more than one check should be taken away during a single lesson.

The student may lose a check in one other way: by failing to return the signed report card by the date set by the teacher. If the student fails to return two reports consecutively, the parent should be contacted.

**Recording the Checks.** (a) The Daily Checks Sheet: The teacher should have this sheet on hand to quickly and efficiently record homework checks and response costs during each lesson. This sheet will also be used to keep track of students who have returned their signed (by parent) report card. As it is returned, circle the "T" for that unit.

(b) The Total Checks Sheet: The teacher will use this sheet to record the total checks earned during each unit. If a reward menu is used, this sheet could indicate whether the student has spent his checks (a slash through the number) or whether he has saved the checks.

15 indicates the student has saved 15 checks;
1̸5 indicates the student has spent 15;
1̸5 8 indicates the student has spent 7, saved 8.

(c) The Report Card: This provides a student with feedback about how he has done on each unit. In addition it is a report to the parents on the progress of the child in the program. The home report will be a powerful management device if the teacher makes arrangements for parents to reward progress at home.

**Primary Reinforcement.** Before starting the program the teacher should explain details of the "check system." Students should know precisely how they can earn or lose checks, and they should know the advantage of earning checks. The teacher will have to make a decision about primary reinforcement, that is, about what the checks can be exchanged for. Here are a couple of suggestions.

(a) A Reward Menu: The teacher (or class) could devise a list of possible rewards to be purchased with a number of checks. Rewards could range from free time to special activity time to material rewards. Here is an example:

*Reward Menu*

| Checks | Rewards |
|---|---|
| 5 | 10 min. free time |
| 10 | 25 min. free time |
| 15 | 40 min. on the computer |
| 20 | comic book |
| 25 | 25 min. free time & comic book |

A reward menu should be carefully put together, considering what is rewarding to the students (it may be necessary to do some experimenting).

(b) Certificates: If certificates are meaningful rewards to the students, they are effective, inexpensive exchanges for the checks. Certificates may be taken home or displayed somewhere in the classroom or school.

**A General Statement on the Behavioral Component.** The aim of the reinforcement schedule is to encourage rather than to discourage. If checks are offered too permissively, they lose their reinforcing power; conversely, if they are administered harshly and critically, children may soon become cynical about them. Praise and encouragement are always a part of any reinforcement schedule. The idea, then, is to be fair, firm, consistent, and "on the side of the child."

## *A Guide for Devising Student Contracts*

In Lesson 16 students are presented with the SAT plan. At this point it may be said that the child has an alternative to overreacting. When faced with an unpleasant event, the child may now choose to overreact or choose to use the SAT plan. Still, using the SAT plan involves some effort and the child may be most comfortable continuing to strive for self-worth in old, destructive ways: attention seeking, power seeking, revenge seeking, assuming a disability. When these problem behaviors become annoying and persistent, the teacher/-counselor is advised to devise a specific intervention: an Individualized Student Contract.

There are two primary reasons for deciding to use a student contract: (1) it allows you to monitor a child's behavior closely; (2) it may become a strong motivator for the child to change his behavior.

Here is a ten-point guide for devising an individualized student contract:

(1) *The pattern of misbehavior should be brought to the attention of the child and the child's parents.* Insist that it is the child's responsibility to stop acting irresponsibly and unfairly.

(2) *Target one or two specific behaviors that you want to change.* For example, if the misbehavior is generally "attention seeking," choose one or two of the attention-seeking behaviors that the child should work at changing. Do not overwhelm the child with vague, broad demands (like "must smarten up" or "must stop acting up"). "Will not interrupt the teacher in class" is a behavior stated precisely and clearly.

It will also overwhelm the child if too many behaviors are targeted at once. One or two is probably all that the child will manage successfully on a single project.

(3) *Agree on a counseling schedule, one or two times per week.* It is most appropriate to inform the parents of the sessions, as well as to tell them about the contract. Even better, the parent could be *involved* in forming the contract.

(4) *During the initial counseling session review the H-B-R model with the child.* Convince the child that he is upsetting himself, he is causing himself to overreact. (It is likely that the child will show some resistance to this suggestion.)

(5) *During the next session review the SAT plan with the child.* Help the child work on some "sensible thinking" to use in a crisis situation. Then work on some alternative plans to overreacting.

(6) *Present the child with a set of rewards for using the SAT plan and punishments for choosing to overreact.* Once again, be precise in describing what constitutes an overreaction. The teacher, of course, cannot always verify if a child has used the SAT plan to avoid overreacting to something. Allow the child to be honest about this; if the child reports that he used the SAT plan, give him credit (providing the claims appear somewhat sincere).

(7) *Be fair and consistent in applying the rewards and punishments.* The contract should be slanted "on the side of the child"; rewards should be given more frequently than punishments. Rewards should be carefully chosen; they should be meaningful to the child. Punishments should likewise be chosen carefully and fairly. A good idea is to have the parents take part in the rewarding and punishing.

(8) *Put the contract into writing.* Sign it; have the child sign it; if the parents are involved, they too should sign it.

(9) *After a reasonable period of time, evaluate the effect of the contract.* Does it need modification? Does the reward schedule need alteration? Are the rewards and punishments appropriate and meaningful? If not, make changes as required and continue. Remember to be positive about the child's efforts and to point out any progress he has made; be on the side of the child.

(10) *At some point you will want to terminate the contract.*

## Devising a Student Contract: A Case Study

The following case study should provide clarification in using RSI and student contracts. Background is provided on an "overreacting" girl who had been taught RSI by her teacher, and the ten steps in implementing her contract are described.

*Background.* Becky was a sixth-grade student in a special education class for students with "general learning disabilities." The class had covered all 25 lessons in RSI and were familiar with the concepts. Becky was familiar with the H-B-R model, with the idea that we upset ourselves from what we tell ourselves, and also with the four-step SAT plan. Still, Becky was not spontaneously using the SAT plan to avoid overreacting.

According to her teacher, Becky engaged in a number of attention-seeking behaviors: she talked extremely childishly to the teacher, continually asked the teacher to look at her work, constantly told on other students in the class, and so on. While these attention-getting strategies were managed by the teacher without too much annoyance, Becky's misbehavior on the playground, at gym, and in the lunchroom had become a significant problem. In these situations she was often involved in fights with the other girls. It was learned that when Becky was rejected — even in very small ways — by another girl, she would punch, kick, push, or swear at her. Often, she had tantrums.

Becky's desperate striving for self-worth was the basis of her attention seeking. Only by getting others to notice and approve of her did she feel significant. Conversely, being ignored was proof that she was an insignificant, worthless little girl. To be left out, laughed at, or teased was a supreme tragedy. It was better to be punished by the teacher than to have others ignore her. Indeed, the punishments would often make her the center of attention and, paradoxically, served as somewhat of a gratification.

When the tantrums on the playground became more frequent, and when traditional punishments did not seem to work, the teacher decided to use RSI and an individualized student contract with Becky. The ten steps are described here.

(1) The teacher met with Becky and explained that her fighting with other students was not going to be tolerated, that it was up to her to stop fighting, and that a number of consequences would follow if she was unable to stop. The teacher explained that she would help her, but that it was Becky's responsibility to act fairly and responsibly on the playground.

(2) Though Becky demonstrated many attention-seeking behaviors, the teacher targeted only two: hurting others in some way and swearing at others. The teacher felt that with her help, Becky could manage this project. The teacher explained to Becky that she must not "swear at anyone," and that she must not "hurt anyone."

(3) At the invitation of the teacher, Becky's parents came in to discuss the problem. Since Becky had a school history of related misbehavior, the parents were very willing to cooperate in any program that might help their daughter.

The teacher briefly explained a few of the key concepts of RSI to the parents. She then pointed out that a contract would be drawn up that would encourage Becky to avoid her attention-seeking overreactions, and to use the

SAT plan as an alternative. The parents agreed to reward and dis( Betty as consistently as possible. The teacher explained that the c( sessions would be twice a week at first, and that the parents would be phoned at the end of each week.

(4) The teacher spent three counseling sessions reviewing the H-B-R model, and trying to establish that Becky was upsetting herself from silly, unproven beliefs she had about others not paying attention to her.

The teacher used the chalkboard to explain the overreactions in terms of the H-B-R.

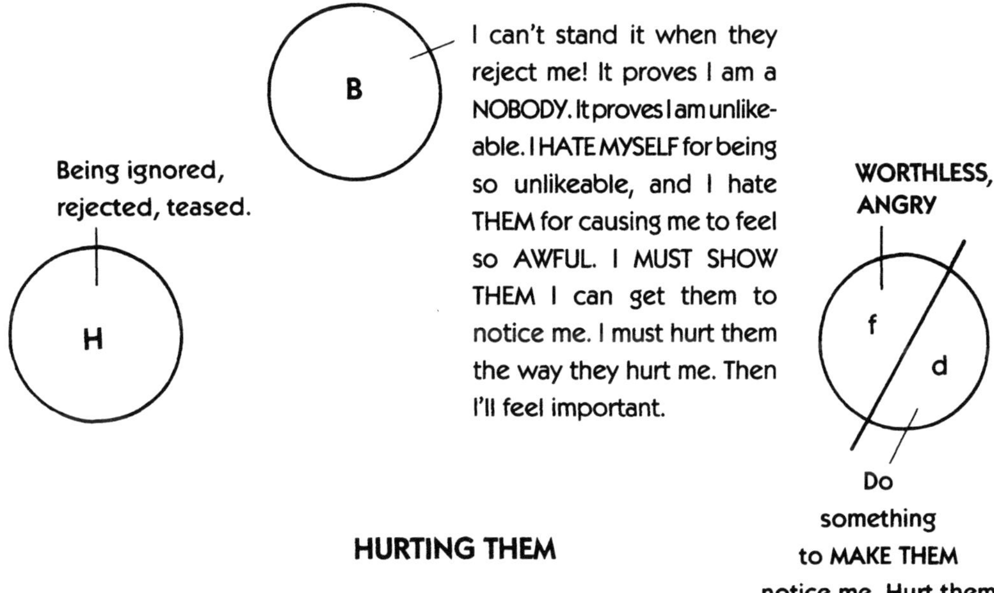


The teacher proceeded to challenge the *silly, unproven beliefs* that were the real causes of the overreactions.

Yes, you *can* stand it.
It proves they may not want to spend time with you sometimes. They have a right to do that. It certainly does not prove no one will ever like you. It never proves that you are a nobody.
Since *they* are not causing you to feel worthless, there is no need to hate them.
Since being rejected does not make anyone a worthless nobody, there is no need to hate oneself.
You do not *need* to show them you can get their attention. Getting their attention won't make you more important, and will likely mean they will want to spend less time with you.
You don't *need* to hurt them.

(5) The teacher then helped Becky design a SAT plan that could be used instead of overreacting. Becky's cognitive skills were limited to handling simple ideas, so the SAT plan was reduced to four simple statements. The teacher role-played situations with Becky a few times, and Becky rehearsed the statements. Finally, she was able to cue in to a "worthless" feeling that was erupting, and apply the following "self-talk."

1. (When they reject me and I start to feel rotten) I say, "Stop. Relax." (I should go away from them for at least five minutes.)

2. (Think sensibly.) I tell myself, "It's OK to be ignored sometimes. It really is OK."

3. (Make a plan.) I will be calm and strong. I will say something nice to them; if they don't act friendly to me, I will just leave them alone.

4. (Reward myself.) I say, "Hey, Beck, way to go."

(6) As the parents agreed, rewards and punishments were to be applied —with consistency — at home. The rewards and punishments were specified for Becky:

Reward: Becky was to receive a reward each time she used the SAT plan to avoid an overreaction to her peers. The teacher felt that she could take the child's word for this: if Becky said she used the SAT plan, it was accepted. Each time she practiced the SAT plan she received a point. When ten points were accumulated, she was to receive a musical tape. (The parents worked this out with Becky; they felt the reward was meaningful to her, and it was something they could easily afford.)

Consequence: Each day an overreaction was recorded, Becky would have to go to bed one hour early. (Again, the parents felt that the discipline was reasonable and meaningful.) An overreaction was recorded if Becky chose to swear at or hurt anyone as a response to being upset.

(7) The teacher phoned the parents each week to talk about the consistency of reinforcement at home.

(8) A contract was drawn up and signed by Becky, her parents, and the teacher. The contract provided space for recording successful and unsuccessful behaviors. In most cases, Becky would record the successful behavior herself; if the teacher noticed an overreaction, she would record it. The contract was kept in the teacher's desk, and Becky took it home each night to show her parents. The contract was established as shown on page *xxviii*.

(9) After each two-week period the teacher and parents met to examine the effects of the contract. Initially (as with most interventions) the contract demonstrated dramatic success. After a "settling in" period of about three weeks, overreactions became more frequent.

It appeared to the teacher that Becky was "forgetting" to use the plan, so she made a point of reminding the student at each recess and lunchtime. "Remember, if you start to become upset, use the SAT plan." The teacher intentionally downplayed any overrreactions (to avoid rewarding attention-seeking behavior) and praised Becky after successful attempts.

After a while the parents and child agreed on a new system of rewards, while the punishment was kept the same.

The teacher put together a graph that compared Becky's baseline preintervention number of overreactions to the number of overreactions during the intervention. The graph illustrates that, although they were always less than the baseline, overreactions were never completely extinguished. Fluctuations usually occurred in response to program modifications.

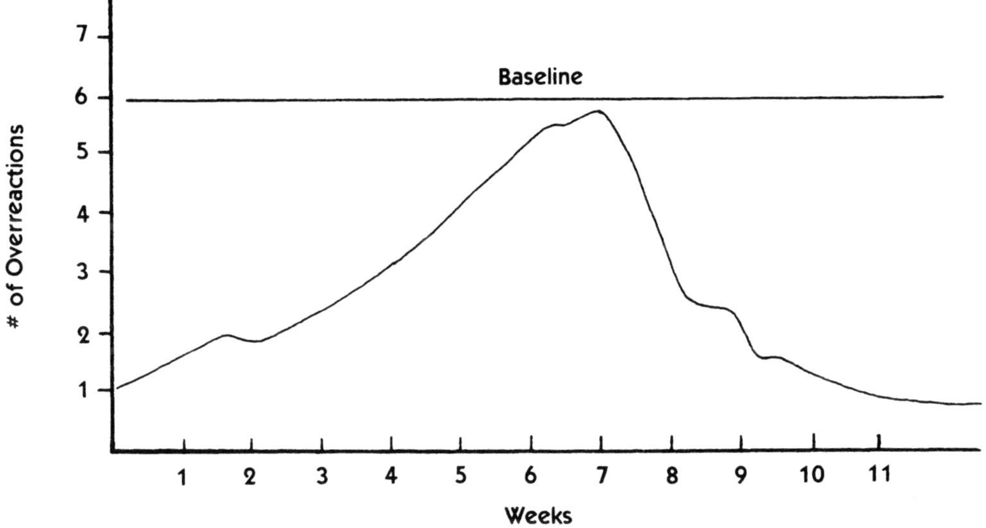


(10) After five months Becky's overreactions had diminished to about one every three weeks. The teacher and parents agreed that intervention had promoted more appropriate behavior. Becky was happy with her success and wanted to try to function without the contract. Parents and teacher agreed to "see how things would go" and terminated the intervention.

It should be reemphasized that there is no "standard" contract for all children; there can only be guidelines. The schedule of rewards and consequences should fit the particular child, and modifications should be introduced as they become necessary. The rule is to keep what works and throw out what doesn't. It is hoped that the guidelines and the case study will provide enough suggestions for any teacher to attempt an individual contract for a "problem child." Putting together a contract, meeting with the child, and monitoring progress require work but are worth the effort.

# Contract

REWARD: 1 point for using the SAT plan.
10 points = 1 tape

CONSEQUENCE: for overreacting—swearing at or hurting someone.
Each overreaction = 1 hour early to bed that night.

I agree to cooperate with this contract:

______________________________ (Student's signature)

______________________________ (Parents' signature[s])

______________________________

______________________________ (Teacher's signature)

| Date | Name of Person Who Upset Me | Did I Use the SAT Plan? | Did I Overreact? |
|---|---|---|---|
| | | | |
| | | | |
| | | | |
| | | | |
| | | | |
| | | | |
| | | | |
| | | | |
| | | | |
| | | | |
| | | | |
| | | | |
| | | | |

# Daily Checks Sheet

Column A: HOMEWORK. Write 1, 2, or 3 for each lesson.

Column B: RESPONSE COST. Write 1 only if the child is extremely uncooperative; subtract 1 in this column if student does not return report card by the established date. When student returns the report card, keep track by writing an "R" in the T (total) column for that unit.

| *NAME* | | *1* | *2* | *3* | *4* | *5* | *T* | *6* | *7* | *8* | *9* | *10* | *T* | *11* | *12* | *13* | *14* | *15* | *T* | *16* | *17* | *18* | *19* | *20* | *T* | *21* | *22* | *23* | *24* | *25* | *T* |
|---|---|---|---|---|---|---|---|---|---|---|---|---|---|---|---|---|---|---|---|---|---|---|---|---|---|---|---|---|---|---|---|---|
| | *A* | | | | | | | | | | | | | | | | | | | | | | | | | | | | | | |
| | *B* | | | | | | | | | | | | | | | | | | | | | | | | | | | | | | |
| | *A* | | | | | | | | | | | | | | | | | | | | | | | | | | | | | | |
| | *B* | | | | | | | | | | | | | | | | | | | | | | | | | | | | | | |
| | *A* | | | | | | | | | | | | | | | | | | | | | | | | | | | | | | |
| | *B* | | | | | | | | | | | | | | | | | | | | | | | | | | | | | | |
| | *A* | | | | | | | | | | | | | | | | | | | | | | | | | | | | | | |
| | *B* | | | | | | | | | | | | | | | | | | | | | | | | | | | | | | |
| | *A* | | | | | | | | | | | | | | | | | | | | | | | | | | | | | | |
| | *B* | | | | | | | | | | | | | | | | | | | | | | | | | | | | | | |
| | *A* | | | | | | | | | | | | | | | | | | | | | | | | | | | | | | |
| | *B* | | | | | | | | | | | | | | | | | | | | | | | | | | | | | | |
| | *A* | | | | | | | | | | | | | | | | | | | | | | | | | | | | | | |
| | *B* | | | | | | | | | | | | | | | | | | | | | | | | | | | | | | |
| | *A* | | | | | | | | | | | | | | | | | | | | | | | | | | | | | | |
| | *B* | | | | | | | | | | | | | | | | | | | | | | | | | | | | | | |

T represents TOTAL CHECKS for the unit. T = sum of A – sum of B

# Total Checks Sheet

Total Checks are recorded here at the end of each five-lesson unit.

Total Checks = Total Daily Checks (from Daily Checks Sheet ) + Test Checks +Bonus Checks (Lessons 16–25)

Put a slash through the total when the student has spent all (i.e., ~~15~~) or part (i.e., ~~15~~ 8) of his checks.

Total Checks
Units

| Name | 1 | 2 | 3 | 4 | 5 | |
|---|---|---|---|---|---|---|
| | | | | | | |
| | | | | | | |
| | | | | | | |
| | | | | | | |
| | | | | | | |
| | | | | | | |
| | | | | | | |
| | | | | | | |
| | | | | | | |
| | | | | | | |
| | | | | | | |
| | | | | | | |
| | | | | | | |

# Report Card

For Unit ____

*Number of homework checks earned:* ________

*Number of test checks earned:* ________

*Number of bonus checks earned (for Units 4 and 5 only):* ________

*Number of checks taken away for being uncooperative or disruptive:* ________

*Total checks for this unit:* ________

Teacher Comment: ________________________________________________

________________________________________________________________

________________________________________________________________

________________________________________________________________

Teacher Signature: ________________________________________________

Parent Comment: ________________________________________________

________________________________________________________________

________________________________________________________________

________________________________________________________________

Parent Signature: ________________________________________________

Student Comment: ________________________________________________

________________________________________________________________

________________________________________________________________

________________________________________________________________

Student Signature: ________________________________________________

# Bibliography


Adler, A. *The Education of Children.* New York: Greenberg, 1930.

Dreikurs, R., Grunwald, B., & Pepper, F. *Maintaining Sanity in the Classroom.* New York: Harper & Row, 1971.

Ellis, A. *Humanistic Psychotherapy: The Rational-Emotive Approach.* New York: McGraw-Hill, 1973.

Kendall, P. C., and Braswell, L. Cognitive-behavioral self-control therapy for children: A components analysis. *Journal of Consulting and Clinical Psychology,* 1982, *50*(5), 672–89.

Keogh, B. K., & Glover, A. T. The generality and durability of cognitive training effects. *Exceptional Education Quarterly,* 1982, 75–82.

Meichenbaum, D. Cognitive behavior modification with exceptional children: A promise yet unfulfilled. *Exceptional Education Quarterly,* 1982, 83–88.

# *Lesson 1: Feelings*

**PURPOSE:** To have students identify and label several feelings.

**PRESENTATION:** Hand out Worksheet 1. Clarify instructions and have students complete the page. Go over the worksheet, having students take turns reading their responses.

**INTEGRATION:** Explain the game "Pantomime":

(a) Each student is to choose one feeling.

(b) Each will be given a turn to pantomime that feeling — to express it with only facial and body gestures.

(c) The audience, then, will try to guess the feeling.

(d) The teacher should take the first turn.

**RECAP:** Have students stand. As each child is called upon, he is challenged to say two feelings; then he may sit. It is not permitted to repeat a feeling said by someone else.

**HOMEWORK:** Project: Look through magazines or newspapers at home to find a person showing a feeling. The feeling should be labeled with a marker, and each student will be called upon to show his or her picture.

Have students note assignment in homework book.

NAME ______________________________ DATE ____________________ 

# Feelings

**Instructions:** Here are a number of feelings. Choose any 12 of them to complete the sentences below.

*Example:* I might feel guilty when I hurt my friend's feelings.

| | | | | |
|---|---|---|---|---|
| upset | interested | angry | guilty | surprised |
| frustrated | excited | afraid | concerned | thrilled |
| happy | loving | shocked | unsure | confident |
| worried | hateful | mixed up | terrified | proud |
| relaxed | annoyed | shy | embarrassed | ashamed |
| calm | bored | glad | depressed | sad |
| astonished | pleased | cheated | insecure | confused |

1. I might feel __________ when ______________________________.
2. I might feel __________ when ______________________________.
3. I might feel __________ when ______________________________.
4. I might feel __________ when ______________________________.
5. I might feel __________ when ______________________________.
6. I might feel __________ when ______________________________.
7. I might feel __________ when ______________________________.
8. I might feel __________ when ______________________________.
9. I might feel __________ when ______________________________.
10. I might feel __________ when ______________________________.
11. I might feel __________ when ______________________________.
12. I might feel __________ when ______________________________.

# *Lesson 2: The Range of Feelings*

**PURPOSE:** To show that feelings may differ in strength, and to show that people will often have different feelings in response to the same event.

**REVIEW:** (1) Have each student say one feeling.
(2) Students and teacher present homework: a picture showing a feeling.

**PRESENTATION:** Hand out Worksheet 2. Clarify instructions and have students complete the page. Go over the worksheet, having students take turns reading some responses.

**INTEGRATION:** Explain the exercise "Confessions": All or some students will be called upon to make a confession when the teacher reads a certain feeling. The student should always begin with "I feel . . ."
*Example:* If the teacher reads "very shy," a response could be, "I feel very shy when I have to ask someone to dance."

The teacher now delivers the following for students to use:

1. very very bored
2. a little angry
3. a little afraid
4. fairly excited
5. fairly frustrated
6. extremely hateful
7. a tiny bit shy
8. fairly guilty
9. a bit embarrassed
10. a little depressed
11. very surprised
12. very very calm
13. happy, happy, happy
14. mildly interested
15. a trifle annoyed
16. outrageously ashamed
17. somewhat glad
18. a bit worried
19. sad, sad, sad
20. quite confident

**HOMEWORK:** Project: to interview someone at home. Using the four-point "afraid" scale, ask that person to say what makes him "a little afraid, mildly afraid, quite afraid, and very afraid." Students should record answers and be ready to report to the class.

Have students note assignment in homework book.

**Worksheet 2**

NAME ______________________________ DATE ____________________ *4*

# The Range of Feelings

Here is a rating scale which could be used to indicate how strongly we might feel about certain events:

| | |
|---|---|
| **1** | **very little** |
| **2** | **some** |
| **3** | **quite a bit** |
| **4** | **very much** |

**Instructions:** Using only the numbers from the above scale, indicate how you would feel about each event presented below.

*Example:* How happy would you be if you were complimented about your looks? If the answer is "quite a bit," you should indicate this by putting a "3" in the bracket preceding the question.

I. Happiness. How happy would you feel about the following?

( ) Getting a new pair of jeans.
( ) Going to England for the summer holidays.
( ) Going fishing instead of having to go to school.
( ) Having someone buy you your own cell phone.
( ) Having pizza for supper.

II. Anger. How angry would you feel about the following?

( ) Someone calling you "stupid."
( ) Having someone accidentally bump into you in the hallway.
( ) Having someone bump into you "on purpose" in the hallway.
( ) Having someone lie to you.
( ) Not being allowed to go outside after supper one night.

# The Range of Feelings

III. Frustration. How frustrated would you feel about the following?

( ) Not being able to figure out a math problem for homework.
( ) Not being able to think of anything to do on a rainy day.
( ) Having your computer "crash."
( ) Not being able to read as well as you would like.
( ) Losing an important game of soccer.

IV. Worry. How worried would you get about the following?

( ) Having an important math exam tomorrow.
( ) Having your mother go into the hospital.
( ) Being sent to the office to see the principal.
( ) Having to say a speech in front of the class.
( ) Having an important soccer game tomorrow.

V. Thrill. How thrilled would you get over the following?

( ) Being told you had just won $50 in a lottery.
( ) Riding on a roller coaster.
( ) Getting a love letter from someone you really like.
( ) Having school called off because of bad weather.
( ) Having someone treat you to a hamburger.

# *Lesson 3: The SAT Pack*

**PURPOSE:** To introduce the SAT Pack; to show that how we "feel" often depends upon "what we tell ourselves."

**REVIEW:** Informal quiz to class (true or false; ask for a show of hands):
(1) Everybody would feel very, very angry if someone bumped into them in the hall. (F)

(2) If it is raining on a Saturday, some may be happy about that, some sad. (T)

Students and teacher present homework: report on the home interview.

Explain to the class that the next 23 lessons will be about students at a school called Hometown High. All students at Hometown High feel bad sometimes. That is true of all of us. But there is a group of students who have learned to act and think sensibly even when something unpleasant happens to them. These students are called the **SAT Pack**. SAT stands for Sensible Acting and Thinking. (You may wish to use the chalkboard to write down these key words.)

*Read to the class:* Hometown High was having a dance on Friday after school. Stewie decided to go, and on the way he met his friend Winston. They decided to go into the gymnasium together. They were both excited as they entered the dance. It was the first dance of the school year, and all of the kids said they were going. To add to their excitement, each of them was secretly hoping that Sally Ann would be there. For the first half-hour they listened to the music and talked to each other. At one point they each got a pop and potato chips. Each of them pretended not to notice Sally Ann, who was talking to some other girls over by the stage.

Finally, Stewie excused himself and wandered over to the stage area. "Would you like to dance, Sally Ann?" he asked.

"No thanks," Sally Ann replied, and kept on talking to her friends.

At that, Stewie picked up his coat and stormed out of the gym. On his way out, he passed Winston and didn't even say goodbye. He slammed the door behind him and started walking home. "It's horrible," he said to himself. "Horrible, awful, terrible. They all hate me. Nobody will ever like me. I'm never going to that stupid dance again. And I'll never ask another girl to dance."

When Stewie finally arrived home he was more depressed than ever. He went into his room, still mumbling to himself, and after five minutes he threw his geography book right at the television set.

Meanwhile, back at the dance, an Oasis song began to play, and Winston decided he would ask Sally Ann to dance.

"No thanks," Sally Ann said, and continued to talk to her friends.

In his disappointment, Winston wandered back to the spot where he had been standing. "Rats!" he said to himself. "I wish Sally Ann had danced with me. Oh well, she has a right to do what she wants, and it's really not the end of the world. I thin I'll ask someone else to dance."

(1) *Ask:* Which boy was obviously a member of the SAT Pack?

(2) Hand out Worksheet 3. Clarify instructions and have students complete the page. Go over the worksheet, having several students read their responses.

> Stress the point that our feelings are often caused by what we tell ourselves. If we tell ourselves it is HORRIBLE, then it feels horrible.

**INTEGRATION:** Have students work in small groups. Appoint a reporter for each group.

Half of the groups are to suppose that Stewie failed a test in school. Each group is to discuss and record statements that Stewie could say to himself in order to get very, very upset. The other half of the groups are to suppose Winston failed the test. Each of these groups should discuss and record statements that Winston might say to himself in order to get a little upset, but not depressed.

Have each group report.

**RECAP:** *Ask:* Why did Stewie get so upset about the unfortunate thing that happened to him? (Stress: because of the things he tells himself.)

**HOMEWORK:** Explain to the students that they have an unusual home assignment. The project is to actually try to upset themselves. They should write down the following details to report:

WHEN did I try this?
WHERE was I?
WHAT things did I tell myself to get so upset?

Have students note assignment in homework book.

NAME ______________________________ DATE ____________________ 

# The SAT Pack

The same thing happened to Winston and Stewie. Sally Ann refused to dance with them. Here is what each boy said to himself:

**Instructions:** Think about the story involving Stewie and Winston, and answer the following questions as best you can.

(1) On the sadness scale rate how sad each became:

| | |
|---|---|
| **1** | **not very** |
| **2** | **some** |
| **3** | **quite a bit** |
| **4** | **very** |

( ) Stewie

( ) Winston

(2) Briefly explain what you think caused Winston and Stewie to feel so differently about what happened to them.

______________________________________________

______________________________________________

______________________________________________

______________________________________________

**Review:** Winston and Stewie go to Hometown High. Winston is a member of the SAT Pack. Do you remember what the letters S-A-T stand for?

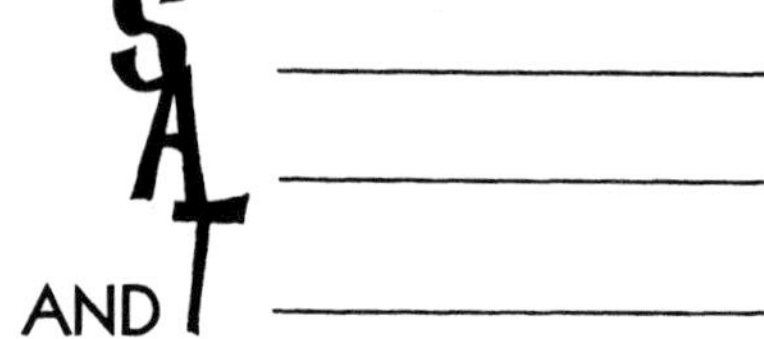


S ____________________

A ____________________

AND T ____________________

# Lesson 4: Overreactions

**PURPOSE:** To teach two rules to distinguish "appropriate reactions" from "overreactions."

**REVIEW:** (1) *Ask:* What is the SAT Pack?

(2) Students and teacher present homework: getting ourselves upset. (Emphasize the statements we tell ourselves to get upset.)

**PRESENTATION:** (1) Here's an opportunity for the teacher to ham it up! Introduce role playing by acting out two separate situations at Hometown High, where first Leanne, then Kim, has her gym equipment stolen. Leanne should be shown to overreact (e.g., whines, kicks the wall, threatens to kill the culprit). Kim should display more appropriate reactions (e.g., is disappointed, plans to report the incident to the office, plans to be more careful).

During the skit the characters should overtly verbalize their thoughts. Leanne would thus tell herself how horrible, awful it is when someone is unfair to her; Kim should remind herself that it is unfortunate to have someone do such a thing but that's the way the world is, and it's really nothing to get overly worked up about.

(2) *Ask:* Who was a member of the SAT Pack: Kim or Leanne?

(3) Hand out Worksheet 4. Have students take turns reading section A. Clarify instructions for sections B and C and have students complete the page. Call on a few students to read their responses.

**INTEGRATION:** Have students work in role-playing groups of two or three. Explain that each group will be responsible for a skit. Each should decide to represent either an "overreacting" student (like Leanne) or one who handles the situation "appropriately" (like Kim). In each skit something unpleasant should happen to the main character.

The audience will watch to see whether the main character overreacts or is like the SAT Pack and reacts appropriately. Encourage the students to think out loud to show what they are telling themselves.

Once the groups have been formed, assign one of the following situations to each group; repeat some if necessary.

| Situation | Show |
|---|---|
| Student is sent to the office by the teacher. | an overreaction |
| Student has to bring home a poor report card to show parents. | an appropriate reaction |
| Student wants to stay out until ten o'clock but his parents want him to be in by eight. | an overreaction |
| Student wants to go to a party on Saturday but her parents do not want her to go. | an appropriate reaction |

After each skit stress: Was that an overreaction or an appropriate reaction? Why? (The reasons should relate to the two rules.)

**RECAP:**

Quiz the students briefly on the two rules for defining an overreaction.

Discuss briefly: If my bicycle is stolen, what could I do to overreact? What might be an appropriate reaction? (The same question could be asked of other situations, e.g., having a pet die, in which case an appropriate reaction might be the expression of a great deal of sadness and grief for a time; whereas the overreaction might be to be depressed for an extremely long time.)

**HOMEWORK:**

Project: From (a) watching a TV program or (b) a book recently read or (c) listening to the news, write down and be ready to tell the class of someone who overreacted. Also, be ready to tell why this was an overreaction.

Have students note assignment in homework book.

NAME ______________________________ DATE ____________________ 

# Overreactions

**Section A:** What is an overreaction? Well, according to the SAT Pack, there are two ways to tell if a person overreacts. Here are the SAT Pack's two rules for identifying an overreaction:

1. if the person gets needlessly upset
2. if the person is unfair to others

**Section B:** In the space below give one example for each rule. In each example tell how a person might overreact.

Rule 1. By getting needlessly upset

______________________________

______________________________

______________________________

______________________________

______________________________

Rule 2. By being unfair to others

______________________________

______________________________

______________________________

______________________________

______________________________

**Section C:** The opposite of an "overreaction" is an " ________

______________________________ reaction."

# *Lesson 5: The H-B-R Model*

**PURPOSE:** To teach the H-B-R Model, a frame of reference for understanding that emotional reactions are caused by beliefs/self-talk.

**REVIEW:**

(1) *Ask:* What are the two rules for deciding what is an appropriate reaction? What is an overreaction?

(2) Students and teacher present homework: someone in the news who overreacted.

**PRESENTATION:** Hand out Worksheet 5. Section A should be used as a basis for discussion; have students take turns reading. Go over the responses. On Question 1 stress that if Sally Ann had been the cause of Stewie's depression, she would also have caused Winston to be depressed —because the same thing happened to both. But she did not! On Question 2 stress that Stewie's overreaction was caused by his beliefs/self-talk. On Question 3 stress that Winston was able to act more sensibly because his beliefs/self-talk were more sensible.

**INTEGRATION & RECAP:** If there is time, here is an integration exercise to supplement the lesson. It may help to use the chalkboard to clarify instructions.

Have students work in groups of three. Each group should plan an unpleasant thing that has happened to Stewie. One of the group members will be H (the Happening), another B (the Belief), another R (the Reaction). As each group presents its statements to the class, it will tell which part of the model is being represented. For example:

**H** "I am H, the Happening. Today Stewie lost all of his school books."

**B** "I am B, the Belief. I believe that it is horrible to have lost my books, and that I am a stupid fool for losing them!"

**R** "I am R, the Reaction. I feel very very guilty and depressed. I go home and cry for five hours."

**HOMEWORK:** Project: This will expand on the project in Lesson 4 (the character in the news who overreacted). Students should illustrate on a blank sheet of paper the H-B-R model of the character. The idea is to make some guesses about a possible happening and belief which could have caused the character to overreact. This should be written down, ready to read to the class.

Have students note assignment in homework book.

**Worksheet 5**

NAME ______________________________ DATE ________________ 

# The H-B-R Model

**Section A:** Do you remember the story from Lesson 3? Stewie and Winston both asked Sally Ann to dance and both got "shot down." Although the same thing happened to both boys, they reacted quiet differently! While Winston was upset, he finally asked someone else to dance. Stewie, on the other hand, stormed home and became violent. What caused them to react so differently? Here is a model to help us understand.

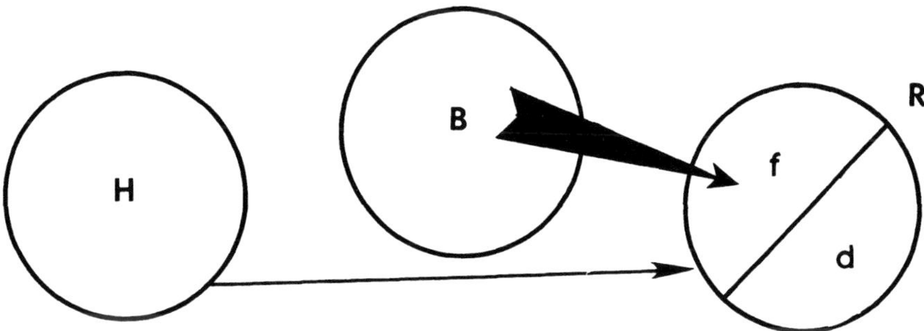


**H** is a happening. It is something that happens to us. It may be a pleasant happening (a new bike!) or an unpleasant happening (getting the bike stolen!).

**B** is our belief. It is something we believe to be true about what has happened to us. It is what we tell ourselves about what has happened.

**R** is our reaction. It is how we react to what has happened. It has two parts: *F* is how we feel; *D* is what we do.

First, let's look at Stewie's H-B-R:

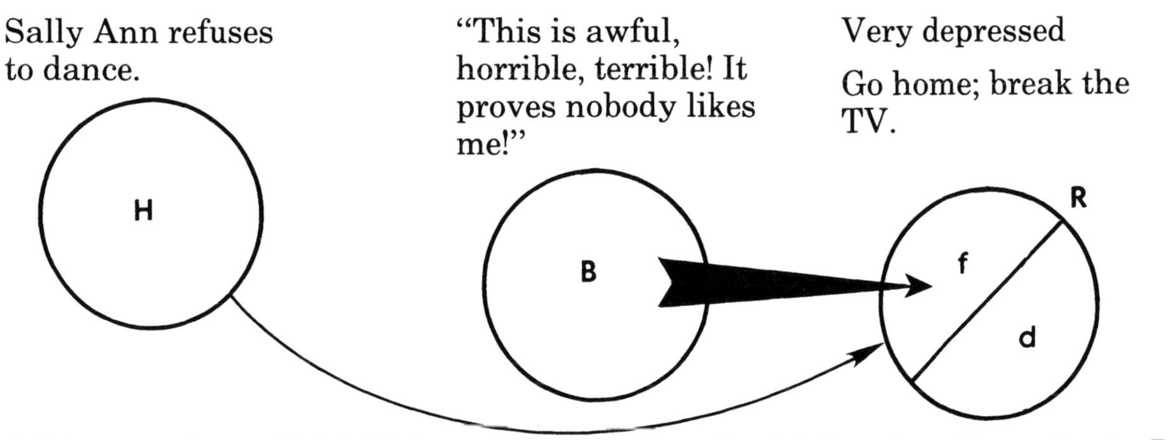


 

## The H-B-R Model

Now, let's look at Winston's H-B-R:

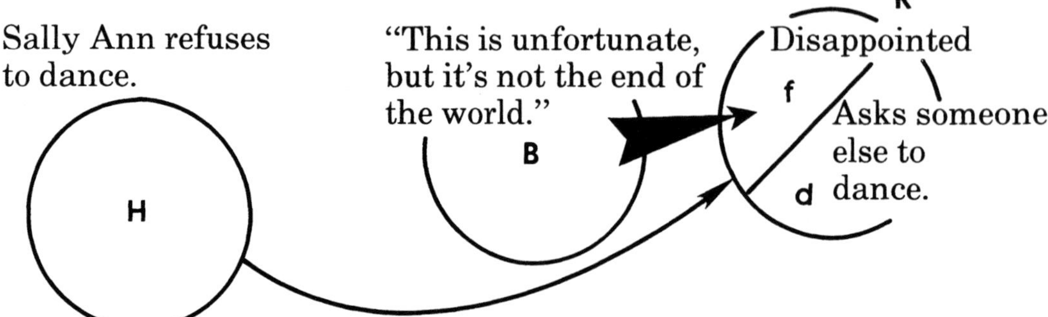


**Section B:** After looking at the H-B-Rs of Stewie and Winston, write down your answers to the following questions.

1. The happening could not have caused Stewie to overreact. Why is this true?

_______________________________________________

_______________________________________________

_______________________________________________

2. What did cause Stewie to overreact?

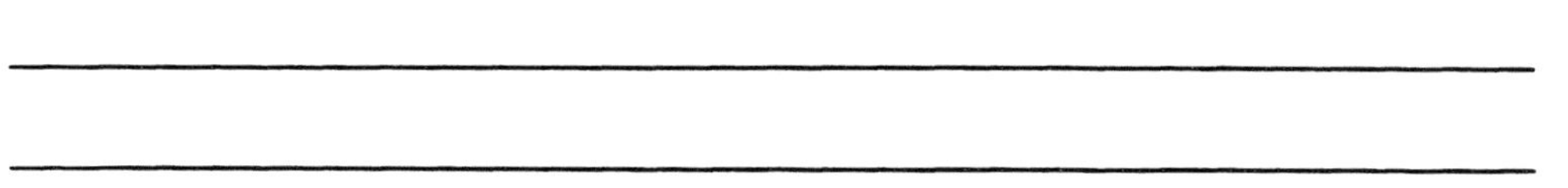

3. Why didn't Winston overreact?

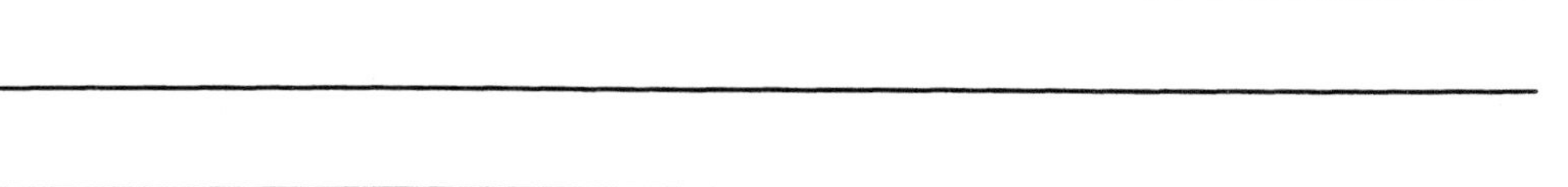

# Unit Test 1

## *For Lessons 1-5*

**Marks**

/4 **1.** TRUE or FALSE? Everybody would feel the same after being turned down for a job. (Circle correct answer.)

/4 **2.** TRUE or FALSE? Stewie usually gets more upset than Winston.

/4 **3.** What are the two rules for identifying an overreaction?

(1) ____________________

(2) ____________________

/4 **4.** Give two examples of an overreaction.

(1) ____________________

(2) ____________________

/4 **5.** The opposite of an overreaction is an " ____________________ " reaction.

/10 **6.** In the H-B-R model each of the letters stands for a word:

H stands for ____________________ .

R stands for ____________________ .

F stands for ____________________ .

D stands for ____________________ .

B stands for ____________________ .

/30 CRITERION TO MOVE ON: 26

B

H

R

f

d

# *Answers to Unit Test 1*

For guidance, see the "Getting Started" section of the introduction under Unit Tests. Each student should achieve at least the criterion indicated.

**1.** False

**2.** True

**3.** (1) getting needlessly upset

(2) being unfair to others

**4.** Teacher will have to evaluate answers here. It may be necessary to have students be specific. For example, getting angry is not necessarily an overreaction, whereas punching someone for bumping into you in the hall should be judged as an overreaction.

**5.** appropriate

**6.** H: Happening

R: Reaction

F: Feel

D: Do

B: Belief

# *Lesson 6: Silly or Sensible — Part 1*

**PURPOSE:** (1) To show three areas of "silly" beliefs which commonly cause people to overreact; (2) to show that silly beliefs cannot be proven true and needlessly upset people; (3) to show that there is a sensible belief to counter every silly belief.

**REVIEW:** (1) With the aid of a chalkboard, review the H-B-R model.

(2) Students and teacher present homework: an illustration of the character in the news overreacting.

**PRESENTATION:** Hand out Worksheet 6. Clarify instructions, then have students take turns reading the examples. Have students complete the page. Go over the worksheet, having students take turns reading their responses.

**INTEGRATION:** Have students put their worksheets away, then call on students individually. After you read one of the silly beliefs, encourage the student to respond with a more sensible version. (Use worksheet examples as reference, or make up similar statements.)

**HOMEWORK:** Explain that we all have silly beliefs. Project: Write down one silly belief that you have and that you would like to change.

Have students note assignment in homework book.

NAME ____________________ DATE ____________ 

# Silly or Sensible — Part 1

A silly belief needlessly upsets us and may cause us to act unfairly towards others. As well, a silly belief cannot be proven to be true.

A sensible belief asks for proof. It allows us to act more appropriately and fairly.

**Instructions:** Here are three kinds of silly beliefs. Under each kind there are three examples, along with sensible beliefs to take the place of two of them. For the third example a space has been left for you to write a sensible belief. Try it!

| SILLY | SENSIBLE |
|---|---|
| **I. You Make Me** | |
| 1. Sally made me depressed. | I depressed myself by telling myself how bad it was that Sally would not dance with me. |
| 2. You make me angry. | I make myself angry by telling myself how awful it is to have been treated that way. |
| 3. The test causes me to worry. | ____________________<br>____________________<br>____________________ |



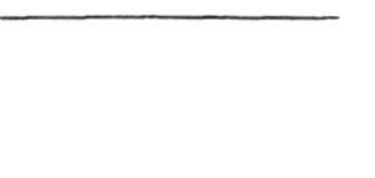

NAME ______________________________ DATE ________________ 

# Silly or Sensible

| SILLY | SENSIBLE |
|---|---|
| **II. "Shouldizing"** | |
| 1. Sally shouldn't do that! | Sally should be the way she is. It would be nice if she danced with me. |
| 2. My parents should let me do what I want. | My parents should be the way they are. It would be nice if they let me do that. |
| 3. If I like you, you should like me! | ______________________ ______________________ ______________________ |

| SILLY | SENSIBLE |
|---|---|
| **III. "Horriblizing"** | |
| 1. It is horrible that Sally wouldn't dance with me. | It is disappointing that Sally wouldn't dance with me. |
| 2. It is horrible to have no money. I can't stand it! | It is unfortunate to have no money. I can stand it, though. |
| 3. It is awful, horrible, terrible to fail. My mom will kill me. | ______________________ ______________________ ______________________ |

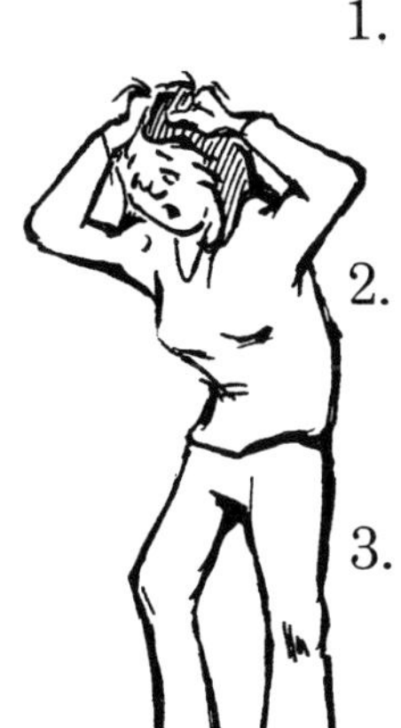

# *Lesson 7: Silly or Sensible — Part 2*

**PURPOSE:** To have the students work with three more areas of silly beliefs.

**REVIEW:** (1) *Ask:* What three silly beliefs were discussed last lesson? (You Make Me; Shouldizing; Horriblizing)

(2) Students and teacher present homework: one silly belief you would like to change.

**PRESENTATION:** Hand out Worksheet 7. Clarify instructions, then have students take turns reading the examples. Have students complete the page. Go over the worksheet, having students take turns reading their responses.

**INTEGRATION:** The integration exercise here is identical to that of Lesson 6. Have students put their worksheets away, then call on students individually. After you read one of the silly beliefs, encourage the student to respond with a more sensible version. (Use worksheet examples as reference, or make up similar statements.)

**RECAP:** Quiz the students to come up with the six areas of silly beliefs. (These could be written on the chalkboard.)

**HOMEWORK:** The last homework exercise had students writing down silly beliefs they'd like to change. The project this time is to write down a sensible belief that would take the place of the silly one.

Have students note assignment in homework book.

NAME ______________________ DATE ______________ 

# Silly or Sensible — Part 2

Here is some more practice in sensible thinking. Below are three more areas of silly beliefs which could cause us to overreact to a happening. For the third example in each area a space has been left for you to write a sensible belief.

| SILLY | SENSIBLE |
|---|---|
| **I. I Need It!** | |
| 1. I need a new computer! | I would really like a new computer. |
| 2. Oh, honey, I need you! | Oh, honey, I want you. |
| 3. I need Sally to dance with me. | ______________________ |
| **II. Putting Yourself Down** | |
| 1. If Sally doesn't dance with me, it proves I'm unlikeable. | If Sally doesn't dance with me, it proves she didn't want to dance with me. I'm still OK. |
| 2. If no one pays attention to me, it proves no one likes me. | Being ignored is sometimes unpleasant, but it doesn't mean people don't like me. I'm still OK. |
| 3. If I don't get even with people who bother me, it proves I am the fool. | ______________________ |

NAME ________________________ DATE ______________ 

# Silly or Sensible — Part 2

| SILLY | SENSIBLE |
|---|---|
| **III. It Isn't Fair** | |
| 1. I can't stand it when my parents aren't fair with me. | I can stand it when my parents don't seem fair. It will be too bad for me, but I'll get over it. |
| 2. People who aren't fair are rotten worms and should be beaten up! | It's nice when people are fair, but they have a right to be the way they are. If they don't seem fair, it's not the end of the world. |
| 3. If I am fair to people, they absolutely must be fair to me! | 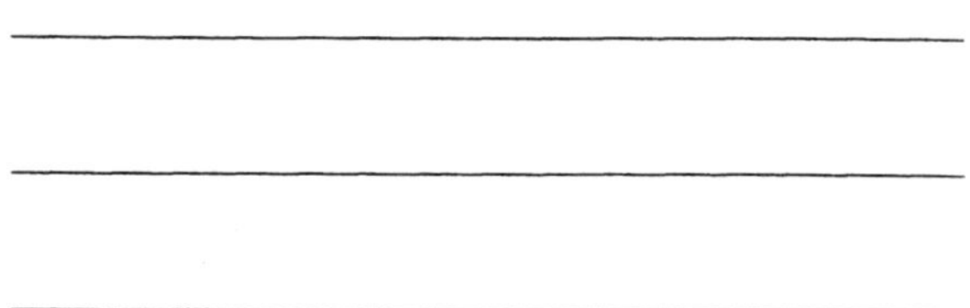 |

# *Lesson 8: Acting Silly*

**PURPOSE:** This lesson will provide further integration of the concepts presented in Lessons 6 and 7. The students will be given the opportunity to actively demonstrate the six categories of silly beliefs which precipitate overreactions.

**REVIEW:** (1) *Ask:* Why is it that when the same thing happens to both Winston and Stewie, they react very differently? (Stress: it is the difference in beliefs/self-talk.)

(2) Students and teacher present homework: one sensible belief to take the place of the silly one.

**PRESENTATION:** Hand out Worksheet 8. Clarify instructions and have students complete the page. Go over the worksheet, having students take turns reading their responses.

**INTEGRATION:** Time for the teacher to ham it up again! Teacher should demonstrate a skit where someone overreacts to some unpleasant happening. The teacher should think out loud to show the silly self-talk that is responsible for the overreaction.

Now the students! Students may individually or in small groups choose a silly belief from one of the six categories, then role-play the scene to show someone overreacting.

**HOMEWORK:** Project: a little memory work! Challenge the students to learn the six areas of overreactions (Worksheet 8 could be used as reference). The students will be given a mini-test next day on this.

Have students note assignment in homework book.

NAME ________________________________ DATE ________________ 

# Acting Silly

**Section A:** Try this review question:

What are the two rules for identifying an overreaction?

1. ________________________________________________

2. ________________________________________________

**Section B:**

Lessons 6 and 7 dealt with six silly beliefs which might cause us to overreact. Here are students at Hometown High who are over-reacting by telling themselves something based on a silly belief. What could these kids be saying to themselves? Read the silly belief above each student, then write the words they might be saying to get themselves upset. The first one is done as an example.

# *Lesson 9: Becoming Sensible*

**PURPOSE:** To give students more practice in changing silly beliefs to sensible beliefs.

**REVIEW:** (1) Have students individually come to the chalkboard and reconstruct the H-B-R model (i.e., one student does one circle, etc., until all circles and letters are complete).

(2) Mini-Test. Hand out a small piece of paper and have students write from memory the six areas of silly beliefs. (Collect, mark later, and hand back.)

**PRESENTATION:** Hand out Worksheet 9. Clarify instructions and have students complete the page. Go over the worksheet, having students take turns reading their responses.

To assist the teacher, appropriate responses to the first two examples on the worksheet are provided. These may be read when correcting the worksheet.

1. If I am nice to him, he must be nice to me. Why must he? A more sensible belief is to say, "It would be nice to have him like me." There is no reason why people should or must like me just because I like them. The truth is it won't be the end of the world if he doesn't like me; I will still like myself.

2. I can't stand it when he laughs at me. The truth is I can stand it; it only annoys me. To be laughed at certainly doesn't mean I'm no good; it merely shows that the person may think something is funny, or he wants to bother me, or that he just likes to laugh. I'm still OK even if 100 people laugh at me; it might be a good idea to laugh right along with them rather than to hate them and get extremely upset.

**HOMEWORK:** Project: Most of us get upset if it rains on Saturday. Write down three ways to entertain yourself when it rains on Saturday.

Have students note assignment in homework book.

NAME ______________________________ DATE ________________ 

# Becoming Sensible

Meet two students at Hometown High. When Lyn is faced with an unfortunate happening, she usually has a silly belief.

Shelly, on the other hand, usually responds with a sensible belief. By realizing that she upset herself, she is able to avoid getting overly upset and acting unfairly. Shelly is a member of the SAT Pack — she does get upset, but she avoids overreacting by taking a few minutes to talk to herself sensibly.

**Instructions:** The left column presents ten silly beliefs. In the right column change each of these to a sensible belief.

| SILLY | SENSIBLE |
|---|---|
| *Example:* I must get people to like me! | Why must I? I can feel good about myself even if some people might not like me. |
| 1. If I am nice to him, he must be nice to me. | 1. ______________________ |
| 2. I can't stand it when he laughs at me. | 2. ______________________ |
| 3. He makes me angry! | 3. ______________________ |

NAME ________________________ DATE ______________ 

# Becoming Sensible

| | |
|---|---|
| 4. It's horrible when it's raining outside. | 4. ______________________ |
| 5. People should not make mistakes. | 5. ______________________ |
| 6. The principal should always be nice to me. | 6. ______________________ |
| 7. Teachers must absolutely be fair all the time; if not they are miserable people and I hate them! | 7. ______________________ |
| 8. It's horrible to be home alone on a Friday night! | 8. ______________________ |
| 9. If someone cheats you, he should be beaten up! | 9. ______________________ |
| 10. I must never make mistakes. | 10. ______________________ |

# *Lesson 10: Jumping to the Wrong Conclusions*

**PURPOSE:** To encourage students to seek proof for their beliefs rather than "jumping to the wrong conclusions."

**REVIEW:** Students and teacher present homework: three entertaining things to do on a rainy Saturday.

**PRESENTATION:** Recount the story of Winston and Stewie going to the school dance (see Lesson 3). *Ask*: Why shouldn't Sally Ann dance with Stewie?

*Then ask*: Is there any way of proving which reason is true? (Although one could try to explore these reasons —for example, by asking Sally Ann —it should be finally established that there was no proof that any of these reasons was true at the time.)

Hand out Worksheets 10a and 10b. Have students take turns reading section A. Clarify instructions for section B and have students complete the section. Have students read their responses. Have one student read section C.

**INTEGRATION:** Have students work in small role-playing groups. The task: plan a skit showing Stewie jumping to the wrong conclusions about something. Stewie should think out loud in each skit. Stress that in each instance Stewie's self-talk was silly and dangerous because it was unproven.

**HOMEWORK:** Project: to think about, then write about, one time you jumped to the wrong conclusion about something.

Have students note assignment in homework book.

NAME ________________________________ DATE __________________ 

# Jumping to the Wrong Conclusions

**Section A:** When there is an unfortunate happening, what does it prove? Well, as you could probably guess, Winston and Stewie usually arrive at different conclusions to that question. After reading this section, can you tell which character is a member of the SAT Pack?

**Happening #1**

Stewie and Winston walk past some of their friends in the hallway. Everyone says "Hi" to each other as they pass, and in a few seconds the friends begin to roar with laughter.

**Happening #2**

Stewie and Winston both had a bad morning. Their mothers yelled at them for no apparent reason.

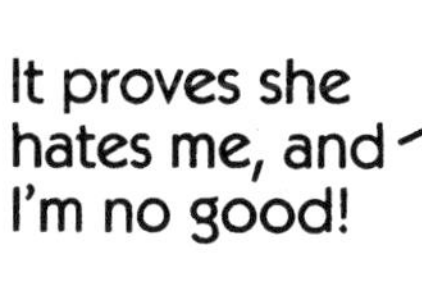

Which character was a member of the SAT Pack? ______________

NAME ______________________________ DATE ________________ 

# Jumping to the Wrong Conclusions

**Section B:** Now it's your turn to try one! In the space provided write another unfortunate happening that someone might have to face. Then draw a simple picture of two characters thinking about the happening, and what it proves. One of your characters, like Stewie, should think silly, unproven thoughts; the other, like Winston, should be a member of the SAT Pack and think carefully and sensibly about what has happened.

**The Happening** **What Does It Prove?**

________________________________

________________________________

________________________________

________________________________

________________________________

________________________________

________________________________

________________________________

**Section C:** Finally, here is a message from the SAT Pack.

"It's easy to jump to the wrong conclusions. We are all afraid the worst will be true. This is why it is important to not jump to the wrong conclusions. Here are four good rules:

1. Tell yourself: Don't jump to the wrong conclusions about this!
2. Ask yourself: What does this really prove?
3. Ask yourself: What other reasons might explain this?
4. Ask yourself: How can I check it out?

NAME ______________________ DATE ______________ 

# Unit Test 2

## *For Lessons 6-10*

**Marks**

/5 **1.** According to the H-B-R model, which idea explains why we might overreact to certain happenings? (Write the word.) ____________

/15 **2.** Change each of the silly beliefs to sensible ones:

| SILLY | SENSIBLE |
|---|---|
| 1. She made me mad. | 1. ____________ |
| 2. I can't stand it when it rains! | 2. ____________ |
| 3. It is really, really horrible if Sally won't dance with me. | 3. ____________ |
| 4. If they laugh at me, it proves I am a fool. | 4. ____________ |
| 5. I need you! | 5. ____________ |

/10 **3.** As discussed in several of the lessons, there are six kinds of silly beliefs. One kind is given here as an example; list as many of the other five as you can remember.

1. You make me!
2. ____________
3. ____________
4. ____________
5. ____________
6. ____________

/30 CRITERION TO MOVE ON: 26

# *Answers to Unit Test 2*

For guidance, see the "Getting Started" section of the introduction under Unit Tests. Each student should achieve at least the criterion indicated.

**1.** Belief

**2.** Answers here may vary and the teacher will have to evaluate them; here are sample answers:

(1) I upset myself by telling myself silly things.

(2) I certainly can stand it when it rains; it's only boring.

(3) It is disappointing if Sally won't dance with me.

(4) If they laugh at me, it probably shows they think something is funny. It certainly doesn't show I am a fool.

(5) I want you.

**3.** (2) "Shouldizing"

(3) "Horriblizing"

(4) I need it!

(5) Putting yourself down

(6) It isn't fair!

# *Lesson 11: Coming to the Right Conclusions*

**PURPOSE:** To encourage students to come to the right conclusions by demanding evidence to support their beliefs.

**REVIEW:** Students and teacher present homework: one time when you jumped to the wrong conclusion about something.

**PRESENTATION:** Hand out Worksheet 12. Clarify instructions and have students complete the page. Go over the worksheet, having students take turns reading their responses.

**INTEGRATION:** Have students work in the same groups as previous day.

Instruct students to plan a skit wherein Winston is faced with the same unpleasant happening that Stewie was faced with in previous day's skit. Winston should be shown to avoid jumping to the wrong conclusions by using his four-point plan. (Remind students that Winston is a member of the SAT Pack.)

**HOMEWORK:** Project: to write about one time when someone you know jumped to the wrong conclusion about something.

Have students note assignment in homework book.

NAME ______________________________ DATE ________________ 

# Coming to the Right Conclusions

What should we do when we're faced with an unpleasant happening? Do you remember the SAT Pack's message?

| | |
|---|---|
| SAY: | Don't jump to the wrong conclusions. |
| ASK: | What does this really prove?<br>What other reasons might explain this?<br>How can I check it out? |

**Instructions:** Read the following happening. Then, write a reasonable response to each of the three questions. Reasonable responses do not have Winston jumping to the wrong conclusion.

## Happening

Several of the kids in Winston's class decided to have a party, but Winston was not invited. He was sad about this, but he decided not to get overly depressed, so he remembered the SAT Pack's message: "Don't jump to the wrong conclusions."

# Coming to the Right Conclusions

| Question | Reasonable Response |
|---|---|
| What does this really prove? | ________________________ |
| | ________________________ |
| | ________________________ |
| | ________________________ |
| | ________________________ |
| | ________________________ |
| | ________________________ |



| | |
|---|---|
| What other reasons might explain what happened? | ________________________ |
| | ________________________ |
| | ________________________ |
| | ________________________ |
| How can I check it out? | ________________________ |
| | ________________________ |
| | ________________________ |
| | ________________________ |
| | ________________________ |

# *Lesson 12: The Funny Papers*

**PURPOSE:** To reinforce the concept that overreactions are a product of silly, unproven self-talk.

**REVIEW:** Students and teacher present homework: one time when someone else jumped to the wrong conclusion about something.

**PRESENTATION:** Hand out Worksheet 12a. Clarify instructions and have students complete the page. Go over the worksheet, having students take turns reading their responses.

There are several sensible responses to the four questions in section B; here are some examples:

1. Getting a low mark in math probably shows that Sandy didn't know those math questions very well. That's all!
2. Failing tests does not mean a person is stupid. Maybe she is not interested in math; maybe she didn't study; maybe she had problems at home; and so on . . .
3. The truth is: If you act nicely to people, they'll probably like you; if you don't, they might not. Students don't normally care too much what their friends get in math. Sandy might get teased, but this certainly doesn't mean the kids won't like her.
4. Sandy might do a couple of things. First, she might ask herself: "Do I hate people for failing on tests?" (Probably not.) Or, she might actually tell the kids about her low mark: she will probably see that she didn't lose any friends over the event.

**INTEGRATION:** Hand out and have the students complete the project on Worksheet 12b.

**HOMEWORK:** Project: to complete the cartoon (started in the Integration exercise) and be ready to read it to the class next day. A suggestion is to construct a bulletin board of the various cartoons.

Have students note assignment in homework book.

NAME ______________________________ DATE ________________ 

# The Funny Papers

**Section A:** Remember the four points of the SAT Pack's message?

SAY: ______________________________

ASK: ______________________________

ASK: ______________________________

ASK: ______________________________

**Section B:** Read the following story from "The Funny Papers." Then answer the four questions on the next page.

## The Funny Papers

3

There—got rid of that. Now nobody will know.

TRASH

4

If they found out I got 40 in math, they would know I'm stupid, and they wouldn't like me, and they would laugh at me behind my back.

1. What did the low mark in math really prove? ____________

______________________________________________

2. Sandy concluded the low mark meant she was stupid. What other reasons could explain the low mark? ____________

______________________________________________

3. Sandy concluded that the other kids would not like her when they found out about her low mark. What is a more sensible conclusion? ____________

______________________________________________

4. Sandy thought: "People will think I'm stupid for getting a low mark in math, and they will not like me." How can Sandy check out these notions? ____________

______________________________________________

**Worksheet 12b**

NAME ______________________________ DATE ____________________



# The Funny Papers

**Instructions:** Now it's your turn. In the four spaces below, create a cartoon sequence that shows someone jumping to the wrong conclusion about something. Don't worry if you're not an artist —very simple drawings will get the point across. Be sure to show your character telling him/herself silly, unproven things.

# *Lesson 13: Who Is More Important—Me or a Rock Star?*

**PURPOSE:** To advance the belief that "we are all equally important because we are humans."

**REVIEW:** Students and teacher present homework: the cartoon depicting someone "jumping to the wrong conclusion." (After the students briefly present and explain their cartoons, they could be used as a bulletin board display.)

**PRESENTATION:** (1) *Read:* Louie had a good seat. It was the first time he had ever been to a rock concert and he was especially happy to be seeing his favorite rock star, Bryan Adams. Throughout the show everyone cheered and clapped, and Louie began dreaming that all the people were cheering and clapping for him. He dreamt that all his friends were in the audience, yelling and screaming and clapping as he was singing his rock songs. If only he could be as important as Bryan Adams!

(2) *Ask:* Why is Bryan Adams more important than Louie? Briefly discuss.

**INTEGRATION:** Hand out Worksheet 13. Read section A. Clarify instructions and have students complete section B. Go over the worksheet, having students present their defences.

**RECAP:** *Ask:* According to the SAT Pack, why is Louie just as important as a famous person? (Stress that we are all equally important simply because we are human beings.)

**HOMEWORK:** Project: to write down one particular skill you have and are proud of.

Have students note assignment in homework book.

NAME ______________________________ DATE ________________ 

# Who Is More Important —Me or a Rock Star?

**Section A:** Here is some sensible thinking from the SAT Pack:

I like Bryan Adams and I really liked the concert, but Bryan Adams is no more important than I am! He may be richer, and certainly more popular—but he is not more important! We are all human beings and therefore are worth the same!

**Section B:** Now it's time for you to put together some sensible thoughts. Show why you are just as important as a famous person.

A. Name a famous person: ______________________

B. What are some things this person has that you do not have?

1. ______________________
2. ______________________
3. ______________________
4. ______________________
5. ______________________
6. ______________________

C. Now here is the tough part: Explain why you are just as important as that famous person!

______________________

______________________

______________________

______________________

______________________

______________________

# *Lesson 14: I Am Not a Mark on a Test — Part 1*

**PURPOSE:** To have the students explore and challenge the destructive self-talk that accompanies failing in schoolwork.

**REVIEW:** (1) *Ask and discuss:* Why are we all equally important?

(2) Students and teacher present homework: one particular skill you have and are proud of.

**PRESENTATION:** *Ask and discuss:* How much do tests and exams bother you?

Tell students to close their eyes while they try to imagine themselves in a test. *Read*:

> You are sitting in class and the teacher announces that everyone is to get ready for the math exam. The classroom gets very quiet and you notice that everyone else seems so calm and confident, especially Sally Ann. She always gets an A in math. As the teacher starts to hand out the papers, you say to yourself: "This is really horrible! I just know I will fail!" You can feel your heart start to pound and you notice that your hands begin to shake. You say: "If I fail this test my mother will kill me!" By now you are reading the test and your heart is racing faster and faster and you are getting a bit dizzy. You can no longer think or concentrate on the questions. You tell yourself: "This will prove I am stupid. My friends will all hate me!" You get so flustered that you decide to put down your pencil and don't even try.

**INTEGRATION:** Hand out Worksheet 14. Clarify instructions and have students complete the page. Go over the worksheet, having students take turns reading the responses they gave for Leanne.

**RECAP:** Draw the H-B-R model on the chalkboard. Have students describe each aspect of the model as it explains Leanne's overreaction to the math test. (Stress that the math test did not/could not upset Leanne; rather it was the self-talk that got her extremely upset.)

**HOMEWORK:** Project: to think about and write down some sensible thoughts for Leanne about her failing the math test. Be ready to read these to the class next day.

Have students note assignment in homework book.

**Worksheet 14**

NAME ______________________________ DATE ______________ 

# I Am Not a Mark on a Test — Part 1

When Leanne sat in front of her math test, she became very very worried. This overreaction was not caused by the test itself, but by silly, unproven thoughts about the test.

**Instructions:** Your job is to read each silly statement, then write a sensible argument against it. To help you get the idea, the first two are done for you.

| Silly, Unproven Statement | Sensible Argument |
|---|---|
| 1. This is really horrible. | Nonsense. Why is it so horrible? The math test is just a few minutes' work. It may be boring or a bit stressful, but it is certainly not horrible. |
| 2. I just know I will fail. | Nonsense. The truth is: I might fail, I might pass. |
| 3. If I fail my mother will kill me. | ______________________________ |

NAME ______________________ DATE ______________ 

# I Am Not a Mark on a Test — Part 1

4. This will prove I am stupid.

5. My friends will all hate me.

6. This proves I'm no good.

# *Lesson 15: I Am Not a Mark on a Test — Part 2*

**PURPOSE:** To simulate a situation in which students practice sensible self-talk.

**REVIEW:** (1) *Ask and discuss:* (a) What causes us to become overly anxious during a test? (What we tell ourselves); (b) Is it appropriate to be concerned about tests? (Of course. Concern will prompt us to prepare for tests, while extreme worry is of no benefit to us.)

(2) Students and teacher present homework: some sensible thoughts for Leanne about failing the math test.

**PRESENTATION:** (1) Tell students to once again close their eyes while they try to imagine themselves in a test situation.

*Read*:

You are sitting in class and the teacher announces that everyone is to get ready for the math exam. The classroom gets very quiet and you notice that everyone else seems so confident, especially Sally Ann. She always gets an A in math. As the teacher starts to hand out the papers you tell yourself: "This is really horrible!" Your heart begins to beat faster. But just then you tell yourself: "Stop, Relax!" You put your pencil down for a moment and you breathe easily and deeply and you tell yourself once again: "Relax." By now the test is on your desk in front of you. You tell yourself: "Be calm, be strong. If I fail, I fail, it's not the end of the world." You pick up your pencil and say: "OK, concentrate, and do your best." When the test is over, you tell yourself: "Hey, way to go!"

**INTEGRATION:** Hand out Worksheet 15. Clarify instructions. Give students a few minutes to study the self-talk that could help them in an exam.

Next have students turn over the worksheet, so as not to see the self-talk.

Now, simulate a test situation in the room. Have the students imagine they are in the presence of an important math exam. (The teacher could even hand out blank pages to create an an atmosphere.) It is the students' task to practice the self-talk that would help them to relax. Following the simulation, *ask*: Were you able to relax? Were you able to concentrate? When is the next time you could practice this "for real"?

**HOMEWORK:** Project: to interview three students from another class: Do tests bother you much? Why/why not? Students should jot down responses and be ready to present next day.

Have students note assignment in homework book.

NAME ______________________ DATE ______________ 

# I Am Not a Mark on a Test — Part 2

Can you imagine yourself in an important math exam? Do you think you could help yourself to relax by remembering to tell yourself a few things? You are going to get the chance to do both.

**Section A:** First, take two quiet minutes to study this self-talk. Then the instructor will help you to imagine you are in an important math test.

Stop. Relax. If I fail, I fail. I'ts not the end of the world. Be calm, be strong. OK, concentrate, do your best. Hey—way to go!

**Section B:** Answer these questions after the simulation.

(1) How effectively were you able to imagine you were in a math exam?

( ) very effectively ( ) fairly effectively
( ) not very effectively ( ) not at all

(2) How relaxed were you able to become?

( ) very relaxed ( ) fairly relaxed
( ) not very relaxed ( ) not at all relaxed

(3) When is the next time you could practice this "for real"?

______________________________

(4) If you try, you should always give yourself credit. "Hey—way to go!" is one suggestion. Can you think of another self-congratulation? ______________________________

______________________________

# Unit Test 3

## *For Lessons 11-15*

Marks

/8 **1.** Kids in the SAT Pack say that we can "jump to the wrong conclusions" if we tell ourselves silly, unproven things. They do not want to jump to the wrong conclusions, so they tell themselves four things.

(1) ______________________

(2) ______________________

(3) ______________________

(4) ______________________

/4 **2.** Give the reason why we are *just as important* as a rock star.

______________________

/28 **3.** **Read** the following statements. If the statement is silly and unproven, mark **"X"** in the parentheses. If the statement is sensible, do not mark anything.

( ) 1. If I fail in school, Mom might get upset for a while.

( ) 2. If I get an "F" in math, it proves I am stupid.

( ) 3. If people find out I fail, they will all hate me.

( ) 4. Mom will kill me if I fail a test.

( ) 5. People don't usually care too much what others get on tests.

( ) 6. I should worry a lot about tests.

( ) 7. It is a good idea to be concerned about tests.

( ) 8. I should become depressed when I fail a test.

( ) 9. It is a good idea to do your best on a test, but not to worry or feel guilty.

( ) 10. Just because I get an "F" on a test, it does not mean I am an "F" in life.

( ) 11. It would be horrible if my friends found out I failed.

( ) 12. It is sad to fail a test, but it's not the end of the world.

( ) 13. I must get people's attention to feel important.

( ) 14. I should not hate myself if others occasionally disapprove of me.

/40 CRITERION TO MOVE ON: 34

# *Answers to Unit Test 3*

For guidance, see the "Getting Started" section of the introduction under Unit Tests. Each student should achieve at least the criterion indicated.

**1.** (1) Don't jump to the wrong conclusions.

(2) What does it really prove?

(3) What other reasons might explain this?

(4) How can I check it out?

**2.** Essentially the answer here is: "Because I am a human being."

**3.**

( ) 1
(X) 2.
(X) 3.
(X) 4.
( ) 5.
(X) 6.
( ) 7.
(X) 8.
( ) 9.
( ) 10.
(X) 11.
( ) 12.
(X) 13.
( ) 14.

# Lesson 16: Hey Guys — Look at Me!

**PURPOSE:** To have students explore the destructive self-statements related to seeking attention and work at changing these statements into more sensible ones.

**REVIEW:** (1) *Ask*: What causes people to overreact? (Stress: What we tell ourselves. If we tell ourselves it is horrible, it will feel horrible.)

(2) Students and teacher present homework: results of three interviews.

**PRESENTATION:** Challenge the students to figure out what is Louie's problem in the following stories. *Read*:

On Monday Louie was in the lunchroom eating with some of his friends. They were all talking about the hockey game the night before and were not really paying much attention to Louie at the time. Louie threw a banana peel at one of the guys, then he laughed and laughed. When the guys continued to talk about hockey, Louie got up from his seat, walked around behind Sammy, and poured chocolate milk all over Sammy's head. Everybody laughed and laughed and Louie felt very happy.

On Wednesday evening Louie and some of his friends were walking up to the shopping plaza. On the way Louie said, "Hey guys, watch this!" When a certain fellow walked past them, Louie pointed at him and said, "Hey, goof, your shoes are untied!" All the guys laughed and Louie felt happy.

On Thursday in gym class everyone was playing basketball. Louie did not like basketball and he was not very good at the sport. All of a sudden he grabbed the ball and started running down the court. The coach blew the whistle and everybody began yelling at Louie. He just stuck out his tongue at the other students. The coach sent him to the office. On the way Louie remembered how he had stopped the whole game and got everybody to yell at him. As he thought about this, he smiled to himself.

*Ask:* (1) In each case what did Louie attempt to do? (get everyone's attention) (2) How do you think Louie felt when he was being ignored? (horrible)

(3) Hand out Worksheet 16. Have students read Section A. Clarify instructions for Section B and have students complete. Read Section C with students.

**INTEGRATION:** Work with a couple of students in the Hot Seat. This is simply a chair placed at a focal position where a student is challenged to apply Winston's plan to fictitious situations. The idea is to get the student to work through the SAT plan to solve the problem. You may have to do a lot of prompting; use suggestions from the rest of the group. (The introduction has a section on "Working with students in the Hot Seat.")

*Situation #1: Read:* You are at a party and everybody is having fun. For five minutes no one seems to be paying any attention to you. You begin to think to yourself: Everybody is ignoring me. They must hate me. I can't stand being ignored. I think I will start showing off and squirt everybody with pop. Then you remember the SAT plan. What do you tell yourself?

*Situation #2.* You are in the lunchroom and some girls are in there also. You think that if you can get their attention they will like you more. At least they wouldn't ignore you. So you decide to tell Sally Ann that her shoes are really ugly. Then you remember the SAT plan. What do you tell yourself?

**RECAP:**

Have students stand. As they are called upon, they are to tell one way Louie could get everybody's attention. As each responds, he may sit.

**HOMEWORK:**

Project: to actually practice being ignored one time. The idea is to be in a situation where several people are talking, and to use the SAT plan to feel good about yourself even when you are ignored. Each student should be ready to tell the class of his experience next day. (To insure homework is completed, students may be required to briefly write down results.)

Have students note assignment in homework book.

At the end of Lesson 16 students should be encouraged to use the SAT plan to avoid overreacting. It is a good idea to talk about this in class discussions and to build the plan into the total discipline policy in the classroom. The students now have a strategy to substitute for misbehavior — though they may not use it! Children will likely have to be encouraged to use the SAT plan. For "problem students" a contract arrangement may work well (see Introduction). If the teacher has utilized the token check system, explain to the students that they can now earn two extra checks if they:

> Use the SAT plan at least 2 times before the next unit test. This will enable them to avoid overreacting and getting into trouble at school or at home.

After the unit test the student will be asked to report confidentially to the teacher on those times the SAT plan was used (the teacher may want to allow some "reporting time" each morning for this as an alternative.) The teacher may ask certain questions, provide feedback, encouragement, praise.

NAME ______________________ DATE ______________ 

## Hey Guys — Look at Me!

**Section A:** Why does Louie try to get everybody's attention? Look at the things he tells himself. Do you think this is silly or sensible thinking?

**Section B:** In today's lesson, you heard several ways Louie tried to get attention. Write down two other ways Louie might try to get attention from people.

(1) ______________________________

______________________________

______________________________

______________________________

(2) ______________________________

______________________________

______________________________

______________________________

## Hey Guys — Look at Me!

**Section C:** When kids in the SAT Pack start to get upset about something, they try not to overreact. They have something; they have a plan! The plan has four steps:

1. STOP. RELAX.
2. THINK SENSIBLY.
3. PLAN... be calm, be strong.
4.

# The SAT PLAN

If I start to feel very bad, and if I am tempted to do something silly and unfair, I try to cool down. I say to myself, Stop. Relax.

Second, I try to think sensibly about what has happened. I try not to jump to the wrong conclusions about what has happened. I remember that this does not mean I am worthless and people will never like me. I remember that I am a good person.

Third, I make a good plan. I tell myself to be calm, be strong. I decide how to solve my problem and feel better by doing something sensible and fair.

Finally, I always remember to reward myself. Even if my plan did not work very well, I remember to say something nice to myself for trying to act fairly and responsibly.

# Lesson 17: I Don't Really Need All That Attention

**PURPOSE:** To give students practice in (1) avoiding attention-seeking behaviors and (2) responding instead with fair and appropriate behaviors.

**REVIEW:** (1) Briefly discuss: Before he started using the SAT plan, Louie would try to feel more important when he was being ignored. What would he do? (seek attention)

(2) Students and teacher present homework: practice in being ignored.

**PRESENTATION:** Hand out Worksheet 17. Clarify instructions and have students complete the page. Go over the worksheet, having students take turns reading their responses.

**INTEGRATION:** Work with students in the Hot Seat. In each simulation the student is prompted to use the four steps of the SAT plan in order to avoid the temptation to act out in an irresponsible attention-seeking manner. When the student in the Hot Seat becomes stuck, allow prompting and suggestions from the other students. (See introduction under "Hot Seat" for specific guidance in this exercise.)

*Situation #1.* Everyone is getting ready to write an exam. You hate exams, and you hate it when no one is paying attention to you. You tell yourself that you will feel better if everyone would laugh at you. You decide to lean back in your chair and "accidentally" fall backwards. But before you do, you think of the SAT plan. What do you tell yourself?

*Situation #2.* You are on a school trip, and everyone on the bus seems to be having fun. You tell yourself that you will be more important if you can be the center of attention, so you decide to run up and pull Sally Ann's hair. But then, you remember the SAT plan. What do you tell yourself?

*Situation #3.* You are in art class and you notice Sally Ann working with a group of girls on an art project. You decide that if you can get their attention you will be more important to them. You decide to go up and ruin their art project and get them angry with you. But just before you do, you think of the SAT plan. What do you tell yourself?

*Situation #4.* You are walking down the hallway and you tell yourself that everyone would think you were more important if you could get their attention. You decide to trip the person ahead of you. Just then, you remember the SAT plan. What do you tell yourself?

*Situation #5.* You are walking by the playing field and you notice some friends playing touch football. You hate being ignored while they are having such fun. You decide to run up and take their football. You think of the SAT plan. What do you tell yourself?

**HOMEWORK:** Project: to once again practice using the SAT plan in a real-life situation in order to avoid getting other people's attention in an unfair way. Write down how you were able to do this and be ready to read it to the class.

Have students note assignment in homework book.

REMIND STUDENTS OF THE OPPORTUNITY TO EARN BONUS CHECKS.

NAME ______________________________ DATE ____________________ 

# I Don't Really Need All That Attention

**Section A:** Louie's class is having a discussion. At least they are trying! Louie is making wisecracks, and getting the class to laugh at him and pay attention to him. But why do you think Louie is doing this? How do you think he feels when no one pays attention to him? In the space below, write what Louie might be telling himself about being ignored.

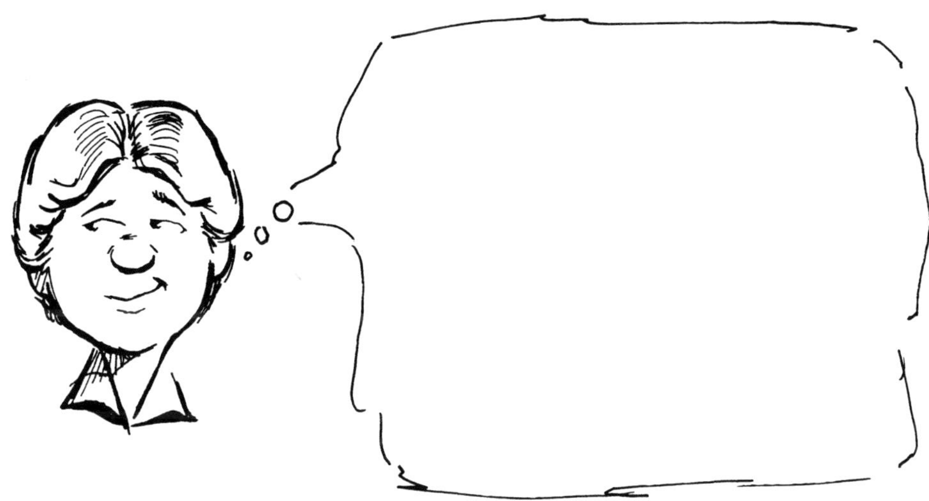

**Section B:** Even kids in the SAT Pack sometimes feel uncomfortable when no one is paying attention to them. But they understand that trying to get everyone's attention is not the answer. They also know that attention-seeking is unfair to others. When kids in the SAT Pack are tempted to show off and to unfairly demand everyone's attention, they remember the SAT plan.

Do you remember the SAT plan? Try to write the four points, in order, of the SAT plan.

1. ______________________________
2. ______________________________
3. ______________________________
4. ______________________________

# *Lesson 18: Who's the Boss?*

**PURPOSE:** To have students (1) explore the destructive self-statements related to power struggles and (2) work at changing these statements into more sensible ones.

**REVIEW:** Students and teacher present homework: practice in being ignored.

**PRESENTATION:** Hand out Worksheet 18. Read the cartoons together. Clarify instructions and have students complete the page.

**INTEGRATION:** Have students work in groups for role-playing. The task: to plan a skit wherein someone is acting in a bossy manner with his friends, and to present the skit.

After each skit stress the need for that character to be the boss; this need is related to his internal dialogue (e. g., I must be the boss or I am a fool).

**RECAP:** *Ask:* Why did Sandy act so bossy? (Stress: from the things she told herself.) Is this silly or sensible thinking?

**HOMEWORK:** Project: Pretend a group of your friends has come over to your house on a Saturday. Everyone has a different idea of how to spend the day. Your assignment is to write down a fair plan the group could use in deciding which idea to accept.

Have students note assignment in homework book.

REMIND STUDENTS OF THE OPPORTUNITY TO EARN BONUS CHECKS.

NAME ______________________ DATE ______________ 

# Who's the Boss?

**Instructions:** Read the above cartoon. Then write a response to this question: How was Sandy being unfair with her friends?

_______________________________________________

_______________________________________________

_______________________________________________

_______________________________________________

_______________________________________________

# *Lesson 19: I Don't Really Need To Talk Back*

**PURPOSE:** To give students practice in (1) avoiding power struggles and (2) responding, instead, with fair and appropriate behaviors.

**REVIEW:** Students and teacher present homework: a fair method for friends to decide what to do on Saturday.

**PRESENTATION:** Hand out Worksheet 19. Clarify instructions and have students complete. Have some students read their responses.

**INTEGRATION:** Work with students in the Hot Seat. In each simulation the student is prompted to use the four steps of Winston's plan in order to avoid the temptation to "talk back" or engage in a power struggle.

*Situation #1.* You are in class and you get up to sharpen your pencil. Just then the teacher tells you to sit down because there is a test going on. You start to tell yourself that it is really horrible to be told what to do, and that you must show everyone that you are the boss. Then you remember the SAT plan. What do you tell yourself?

*Situation #2.* You are walking down the hallway with some of your friends. You meet a teacher in the hall and he tells you to get rid of your gum. You begin to think that you must show this teacher and your friends that you are important by getting into an argument with the teacher. But before you say anything, you remember the SAT plan. What do you tell yourself?

*Situation #3.* You forgot to do your homework, and the teacher explains that you must come in after school to finish it. You tell yourself that you can't stand it when a teacher tells you what to do in front of the whole class. You decide that you must show everybody who is the boss by talking back to the teacher. Just then, you remember the SAT plan. What do you tell yourself?

*Situation #4.* You are at the dinner table. You explain to your mother that you would like to go outside and have fun after the meal. Your mother says that it is quite all right, but you must be in the house by 7:30. You want to prove to your mother that you can be as important as she is, and the only way to do this is to "talk back" to her. You must show her that you are the boss. But before you say anything, you remember the SAT plan. What do you tell yourself?

*Situation #5.* You are in gym class. One of the rules for gym is to have your shorts on for class, but you left them at home. The gym teacher says that today you may not participate in basketball. Since he was telling you what to do in front of the whole class, you decide that you must prove that you are just as important as the teacher. You tell yourself that if you don't show everyone who is the boss, you will be the fool. You decide to get into an argument with him. But then, you think about the SAT plan. What do you tell yourself?

Briefly discuss: Do you think it is possible to feel good about ourselves when someone tells us what to do?

**HOMEWORK:** Project: to put the SAT plan to work at home. The next time your parent tells you to do something and you want to talk back and show you are the boss, you are to think of the SAT plan. You must try not to talk back and to feel good about yourself. The details should be written down so they can be read to the class.

Have students note assignment in homework book.

REMIND STUDENTS OF THE OPPORTUNITY TO EARN BONUS CHECKS.

NAME ______________________ DATE ______________ 

# I Don't Really Need To Talk Back

**STORY 1**

Read the first two frames of the story. Since Sandy makes silly, unproven statements to herself, she will probably overreact. In the final frame write what Sandy will likely say to her father.

**STORY 2**

Read the first two frames of this story. Kim is a member of the SAT Pack. Since she tries to think sensibly, she will avoid an overreaction. In the final frame write what Kim will likely say to her father.

# *Lesson 20: Getting Even*

**PURPOSE:** To have students (1) explore the destructive self-statements related to acts of revenge and (2) work at changing these statements into more sensible ones.

**REVIEW:** Students and teacher present homework: one attempt at using the SAT plan to avoid "talking back."

*Ask:* Does the plan become easier to use the more often it is used? Discuss.

**PRESENTATION:** Hand out Worksheet 20. Clarify instructions and have students complete the page. Go over the worksheet, having some students read responses.

**INTEGRATION:** Have students work in groups for role-playing. The task is to plan a skit wherein someone thinks he has to get even with someone, then to present the skit.

After each skit, stress that the character's need to get even is related to his internal dialogue (e.g., I must get even or I am a fool).

**RECAP:** *Ask:* Why did Dewey have to get even? (Stress: his thinking is silly; he reasons that if he doesn't get even, he is made a fool; he must continually get back at people in order to respect himself.)

**HOMEWORK:** Project: Pretend you are in a game of soccer and someone comes up and gives you a good hard check. Write down some fair, sensible thinking about what has happened to you.

Have students note assignment in homework book.

| REMIND STUDENTS OF THE OPPORTUNITY TO EARN BONUS CHECKS. |
|---|

NAME ______________________________ DATE ____________________ 

# Getting Even

**Section A:** Review: Write the four steps of the SAT plan.

1. ______________________________
2. ______________________________
3. ______________________________
4. ______________________________

**Section B:** Here is a story about a soccer game at Hometown High.

Dewey was a very good soccer player. He was excited the day his team was to compete for Hometown High's championship trophy. But the other team had the "new kid," who was also supposed to be very good! When Dewey dribbled the ball down the field, the new kid easily took the ball from him, then went down the field and scored. "That new kid made me look like a fool!" Dewey said to himself. "I must get back at him or else I will look bad!" At that, Dewey went up to the new kid and punched him.

**Instructions:** Examine Dewey's "self-talk." Do you think the statements were silly or sensible? Explain your choice.

______________________________

______________________________

______________________________

______________________________

______________________________

______________________________

______________________________

______________________________

______________________________

# Unit Test 4

## *For Lessons 16-20*

**Marks**

/18 **1.** Winston's thinking is usually fair and sensible. Stewie's thinking is usually silly and unproven.

Read the following "thoughts." If it is Winston's thought, mark "W" in the bracket. If it is Stewie's thought, mark "S" in the bracket.

(a) If I am ignored, it does not mean people don't like me. I can learn to be calm and strong. (   )

(b) It is horrible if someone upsets me. People should always be nice to me. (   )

(c) When the teacher tells me what to do, I don't need to talk back to prove I am the boss. (   )

(d) I can't stand it when someone tells me what to do! (   )

(e) Attention is sometimes nice. But I feel important even when no one is paying attention to me. (   )

(f) People should always be nice to me. When they're not, I will get even with them. (   )

(g) Sometimes people will tell me what to do. That's OK. It does not mean I am a fool. (   )

(h) You should always get even with people who bother you, or else you are a fool! (   )

(i) It's OK to be friendly with people, even if they are not friendly with you. (   )

/12 **2.** Write the four points of the SAT plan.

(1) ______________________________

(2) ______________________________

(3) ______________________________

(4) ______________________________

/30 CRITERION TO MOVE ON: 26

BONUS CHECKS: Allow students to report on two instances where they practiced the SAT plan.

# *Answers to Unit Test 4*

For guidance, see the "Getting Started" section of the introduction under Unit Tests. Each student should achieve at least the criterion indicated.

**1.** (a) (W) (b) (S) (c) (W)

(d) (S) (e) (W) (f) (S)

(g) (W) (h) (S) (i) (W)

**2.** (1) Stop. Relax.

(2) Think sensibly.

(3) Make a plan . . . be calm, be strong.

(4) Congratulate.

# *Lesson 21: I Don't Really Need To Get Even*

**PURPOSE:** To give students practice in (1) avoiding acts of revenge and (2) responding instead with fair and appropriate behaviors.

**REVIEW:** Students and teacher present homework: one fair and sensible way to think about a soccer check.

**PRESENTATION:** Hand out Worksheet 21. Clarify instructions and have students complete the page. Go over the worksheet, having some students read responses.

**INTEGRATION:** Work with students in the Hot Seat. In each simulation the student is prompted to use the four steps of the SAT plan in order to avoid the temptation to "get even" with people who may frustrate him.

*Situation #1.* You are in art class. You don't like the art project and you decide not to participate. The teacher then tells you to get to work or leave the room. You begin to get very angry inside and you tell yourself that you must get even with this teacher for singling you out in class. But before you act, you remember the SAT plan. What do you tell yourself?

*Situation #2.* You are out on the school grounds. For some reason you walk up and kick a ball that belongs to a group of other children. The teacher sees you, comes over, and tells you that you have a detention after school. You tell yourself that you must get back at this no-good teacher for doing this to you. Then you remember the SAT plan. What do you tell yourself?

*Situation #3.* You are on the city bus. When you begin to talk loudly, the bus driver tells you to be quiet. You tell yourself: "That no-good bus driver made a fool out of me in front of everybody. I will hurt his feelings by calling him a name." Then you remember the SAT plan. What do you tell yourself?

*Situation #4.* The principal sees you fooling around in the hallway. He tells you to sit in the office. You say to yourself: "I hate people who boss me around. When he hurts my feelings it proves to everybody that he is the big shot and I am the fool. I will get back at him and hurt his feelings, then I won't be the fool." Then you remember the SAT plan. What do you tell yourself?

*Situation #5.* You get out of your seat to sharpen your pencil. "Sit down!" the teacher tells you. Immediately you begin thinking of a way to get even with the teacher for making a fool out of you in front of everyone. You decide to call the teacher a name in front of everyone so you won't be the fool anymore. Then you remember the SAT plan. What do you tell yourself?

**RECAP:** Briefly discuss: Do you think it is possible to feel good about ourselves if we don't get even with someone who may be unfair with us?

**HOMEWORK:** (1) Project: (i) to write down one thing that an adult might do to make you want to get even with him; and (ii) to write down one thing you could tell yourself to be less upset when an adult might do this.

Have students note assignment in homework book.

| REMIND STUDENTS OF THE OPPORTUNITY TO EARN BONUS CHECKS. |
| --- |

NAME ______________________________ DATE ________________ 

# I Don't Really Need To Get Even

**Section A:** Stewie's teacher noticed that he was continually trying to disrupt a class discussion. The teacher then told Stewie to stand out in the hall so the class could continue the discussion. Stewie became very very angry. He became hot and his eyes glared at the teacher. He wanted to get back at the teacher, to hurt the teacher's feelings in some way.

Why do you think Stewie starts feeling this way? Why do you think he must get even in order to respect himself? In the space below write what Stewie might be telling himself about getting back at that teacher.

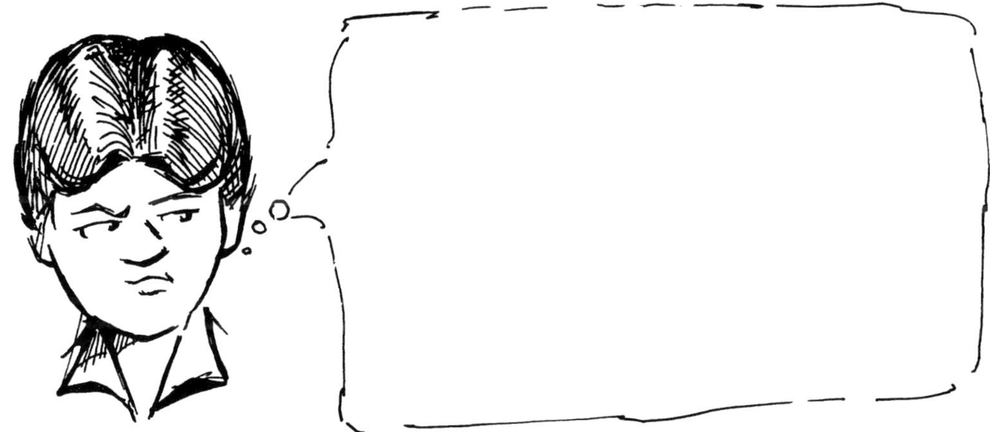

**Section B:** Stewie, of course, feels that he absolutely must get back at anyone who hurts his feelings. Help him out. How can a person respect himself without always having to get even? What is some sensible thinking about this?

______________________________________________

______________________________________________

______________________________________________

______________________________________________

______________________________________________

______________________________________________

______________________________________________

# *Lesson 22: Giving Up*

**PURPOSE:**

To have students (1) explore the destructive self-statements related to feelings of failure and giving up, and (2) work at changing these statements into more sensible ones.

**REVIEW:**

Students and teacher present homework: (1) one thing an adult does that makes you want to get back at that person; (2) one thing you could tell yourself to be less upset about this.

**PRESENTATION:**

*Read*:

Winston and Stewie went to the school dance.

"Are you going to ask Sally Ann to dance?" Winston asked Stewie.

"No, I don't like dancing. Besides, I don't like Sally Ann, either." Stewie answered.

"Well," Winston said, "This is really nervy for me, but I think I'll go ask her."

In a few minutes Winston returned. "Well, did she dance with you?" Stewie asked. "No," said Winston sadly. "I wish she would have, I really like her, but she didn't."

"So what are you going to do now?" Stewie asked his friend.

"Oh," said Winston, "I think I'll just ask someone else."

"Well, what if she won't dance either?" Stewie asked.

"Disappointing," Winston said, "but not the end of the world."

"Won't you feel stupid?" Stewie asked.

"Why should I?" said Winston. "Someone not dancing with me doesn't prove I'm a jerk."

"Well," said Stewie, not quite understanding his friend, "Doesn't it make you want to punch a girl when she says she doesn't want to dance?"

"Of course not!" Winston replied. "She has a right not to dance with me."

"But she makes you look like a real fool!" said Stewie.

"Well," said Winston, "You only feel like a fool if you tell yourself you are a fool. I tell myself that it is OK if a girl says no. I tell myself that it is good to ask, even if she says no."

"But didn't you even call her a name when she said no?" Stewie asked.

"Of course not!" said Winston. "I said, 'Thanks anyway, Sally Ann.' "

Stewie just walked away. He surely could not understand his friend.

Hand out Worksheet 22. Clarify instructions and have students complete the page. Go over the worksheet, having students read responses.

**INTEGRATION:** Have students work in groups for role-playing. The task is to plan a skit wherein Stewie gives up at something (e.g., trying out for a team, writing a test), then to present the skit.

After each skit stress Stewie's fear of trying and his probable logic: It is horrible to fail; it means I'm no good.

**RECAP:** *Ask:* Why is Stewie afraid to try things? (Stress: from the things he tells himself.)

**HOMEWORK:** Project: to write down and be ready to report on one thing you have given up on over the last two months.

Have students note assignment in homework book.

REMIND STUDENTS OF THE OPPORTUNITY TO EARN BONUS CHECKS.

NAME ______________________________ DATE ________________ 

# Giving Up

Stewie has reasoned that it is best to play things safe! If you don't take any chances, you can't get hurt. So he doesn't really study for his math test — if he studies and fails, he believes he must be completely stupid. He doesn't try out for a team unless he is absolutely certain he will make it. He doesn't try in school, he doesn't ask Sally Ann to dance. He always plays it safe.

I'm not even going to try. I will just fail anyway, and that proves I'm no good.

What is wrong with Stewie's beliefs?

______________________________________________

______________________________________________

______________________________________________

What do you think Winston would think?

______________________________

______________________________

______________________________

Last, answer this question: If you try something and fail, what does it prove?

______________________________________________

______________________________________________

______________________________________________

______________________________________________

# *Lesson 23: Trying*

**PURPOSE:** To encourage students to take risks rather than "give up" on potentially rewarding experiences.

**REVIEW:** Teacher and students present homework: one thing you have given up on over the last two months.

**PRESENTATION:** Hand out Worksheet 23. Clarify instructions and have students complete the page. Go over the worksheet, having students read responses.

**INTEGRATION:** Work with students in the Hot Seat. In each simulation the student is prompted to use the four steps of the SAT plan in order to avoid the temptation to give up on potentially rewarding experiences.

*Situation #1.* You are reading a notice put up on the bulletin board beside the gym doors: "Basketball tryouts tonight." You tell yourself that there is no sense in even trying out for basketball. You will just fail, and that will show everyone how stupid and no good you are. Then you remember the SAT plan. What do you tell yourself?

*Situation #2.* You are at the school dance. You see someone you'd like to dance with, but you tell yourself she probably won't dance anyway. You tell yourself: "If I ask her and she says no, that proves I'm no good and no one likes me." You decide never to ask anyone to dance. Just then, you remember the SAT plan. What do you tell yourself?

*Situation #3.* You are about to take a math test. You tell yourself that you will just fail anyway. When you fail, it proves how stupid you are, and that means you are a no-good whom no one should ever like. You decide it is better to not even try, so people can't say you are stupid. Then you remember the SAT plan. What do you tell yourself?

*Situation #4.* A spelling contest! Side 1 against Side 2. Everybody is excited, but you say to yourself: "I hate these things. If I goof up on a word, I will show everyone how stupid and no-good I really am. I am not going to try." Then you remember the SAT plan. What do you tell yourself?

*Situation #5.* You are in gym class and everyone is playing volleyball. You tell yourself that if the ball comes to you, you will miss it, and everybody will laugh at you. It will prove you are a stupid no-good and you should hate yourself for being so awful. You decide to just goof around and not even try if the ball comes to you. Then you remember the SAT plan. What do you tell yourself?

**RECAP:** *Ask:* Do you really think it's possible to feel good about ourselves even when we fail at some things? Does failing at one thing make you a total failure in life?

**HOMEWORK:** Project: to think about and be ready to report one thing you promise yourself to try over the next month.

Have students note assignment in homework book.

| REMIND STUDENTS OF THE OPPORTUNITY TO EARN BONUS CHECKS. |
|---|

NAME ______________________________ DATE ________________ 

# Trying

**Lynn**

If I fail at something, it only proves i'm a stupid **no-good**! It's better to not even try!

**Dusty**

Failing at **some** things doesn't prove I'm a **total failure**. It's better to take a chance sometimes.

Lynn always plays it safe! She doesn't want to risk failing, because she thinks that if she fails at something, it proves she is a total failure in life. So she thinks it is better to not even try. Dusty is a SAT Pack member. When he tries out for something, he is a bit nervous, but he remembers something important: failing does not mean you are a worthless person. He knows that it is OK to fail. He still likes himself even if he fails. So, Dusty sometimes takes chances. He risks failing, because he knows that even if he fails, he is still a good person.

NAME ______________________________ DATE ________________ 

## Trying

**Instructions:** There are some things in life that involve risk. If you try and are successful, it would be good for you. No one should take foolish risks, but some risks are good to take. Think about some good, healthy risks that a person might take. Then write the two possible decisions that a person might make about this risk. The first one is done as an example.

| | Giving Up | Trying |
|---|---|---|
| 1 | You think you might have a chance at trying out for the school basketball team. But you don't want to risk not making it because it would "show everybody you are not so hot at basketball and that would mean you are totally worthless." | You sign up for the tryouts, work very hard in the tryouts, and show up for all practices. You give yourself credit for trying and remember that it is not such a big deal if you don't make the team — at least you tried! |
| 2 | | |
| 3 | | |

# Lesson 24: Changing

**PURPOSE:** (1) To provide a summary of the last six lessons; (2) to give students additional practice in thinking sensibly and acting appropriately.

**REVIEW:** (1) Have students review the SAT plan.

(2) Students and teacher present homework: one new thing you vow to try.

**PRESENTATION:** Hand out Worksheet 24. Clarify instructions and have students complete the page. Go over the worksheet, having students read responses.

**INTEGRATION:** Have students work in groups for role-playing. The task is to plan and present a skit that shows how an overreacting student could have changed since she began using the SAT plan.

Each group is to be assigned one of the following situations:

1. You are in math class and someone hits you with a spitball.
2. The teacher yells at you for something.
3. Everyone in class is ignoring you.
4. In class, someone punches you and the teacher does not notice it.
5. Someone accidentally bumps into you in the hallway.

In each skit the character should "think out loud" to show that he is reacting sensibly and using the SAT plan.

**HOMEWORK:** Project: to write up and be ready to report the one behavior that (you think) has gotten you into most trouble (a) with teachers, and (b) with your parent(s).

Have students note assignment in homework book.

REMIND STUDENTS OF THE OPPORTUNITY TO EARN BONUS CHECKS.

**Worksheet 24**

NAME ______________________ DATE ______________ 

# Changing

Stewie used to get into a lot of trouble at school. The four ways of getting into trouble are listed below. Write in one example for each of the ways.

| What Way? | An Example |
|---|---|
| Trying to get everybody's attention. | ______________________ |
| Talking back to the teacher. | ______________________ |
| Trying to make the teacher feel bad. | ______________________ |
| Not trying. | ______________________ |

# Changing at Hometown High

It has taken some time, but many of the students at Hometown High have changed. They have joined the SAT Pack. How have they changed? Read the following:

They now use the SAT plan to avoid overreacting and to be fairer to others.

They are not perfect, but they are much more responsible.

The teachers like their behavior better, the other students like their behavior better, their parents like their behavior better.

Most important — they are happier with their own behavior.

They no longer need to act up or give up to feel good about themselves.

The more they practice the SAT plan, the easier it is, and the better they become.

# Lesson 25: Getting the Rules Straight

**PURPOSE:** (1) To emphasize the importance of knowing precisely what the rules are; (2) to demonstrate a procedure for disagreeing with an adult.

**REVIEW:** Students and teacher present homework: one behavior that has gotten you into trouble with (a) teachers, and (b) parents.

**PRESENTATION:** Hand out Worksheet 25. Clarify instructions to section A and have students complete. Go over section A, having students put one hand up if they were sure of the rule, two if they were not sure. Read section B.

**INTEGRATION:** Have students work in role-playing groups. The task: to show in a skit how to effectively disagree with an adult — specifically by following the three steps suggested in section B of the Worksheet. Here are some suggestions for the students: your duties in your bedroom at home; you got into trouble in class, but it wasn't your fault; you would like to stay out an hour later tonight to be with your friends; someone in the class keeps bothering you.

*Stress*: in each of the situations there is an appropriate, fair way to talk with adults. Although the three-step procedure will rarely get the young person into trouble, it will not always allow people to get what they want. But at least you tried to be fair and honest, and you should congratulate yourself for that!

**HOMEWORK:** Project: to schedule a talk with someone at home, and to show that you have followed the three steps.

Have students note assignment in homework book.

This final lesson might be an introduction to social skills training. From this point the teacher could plan role-playing lessons in which the students practice other specific social skills. Have you noticed very definite behaviors that students could work at changing?

An idea is to make a list of situations where students could benefit from practice in acting appropriately. Then, have students role-play these situations; follow-up discussion should evaluate the appropriateness of the behavior. Students in the audience could volunteer alternate behaviors for dealing with the problem in an appropriate way.

For example: some students continually interrupt the teacher. An idea is to discuss appropriate ways to interrupt, then to act these out in mini-skits.

The students may also want to generate a list of "problem situations" and then to role-play them.

NAME ________________________________ DATE ________________ 

# Getting the Rules Straight

**Section A:** Why do young people get into trouble at home and school? As the previous lessons have pointed out, part of the reason lies with our self-talk — the silly, unproven things we tell ourselves that cause us to overreact. But part of the reason may be that we are not sure of the rules.

**Instructions:** Here is a brief quiz. Are you absolutely sure of each of the following rules? Read each and check the appropriate response.

| Not Sure | Am Sure | |
|---|---|---|
| ( ) | ( ) | 1. The exact time you are expected to come into the house on a school night. |
| ( ) | ( ) | 2. The exact time you must come into the house on a Saturday evening. |
| ( ) | ( ) | 3. In this class are you allowed to get a drink of water without asking? |
| ( ) | ( ) | 4. At home, what will happen if you come in late on a school night? |
| ( ) | ( ) | 5. Are you allowed to sharpen your pencil in this class without asking first? |
| ( ) | ( ) | 6. What happens if you are late for school? |
| ( ) | ( ) | 7. What are you to do if you disagree with something the teacher has said? |
| ( ) | ( ) | 8. What are you to do if you disagree with something your parent has said? |
| ( ) | ( ) | 9. What will happen if you are late for school three times? |
| ( ) | ( ) | 10. Exactly what duties do you have at home? |
| ( ) | ( ) | 11. Exactly when are the duties to be done? |
| ( ) | ( ) | 12. The words you are not to use in the classroom. |
| ( ) | ( ) | 13. The rules of the school playground. |
| ( ) | ( ) | 14. The rules of the school library. |

 

## Getting the Rules Straight

**Section B.** Do you know how to disagree? As pointed out, many young people overreact when they happen to disagree with an adult, but it is possible to disagree and not overreact. If you do this, there probably won't be much trouble!

*Step 1:* Politely ask for a time to have a talk.

*Step 2:* When you finally have your talk, state your concern politely. Tell the person honestly how you feel about what has happened, or about what is happening.

*Step 3:* Thank the person.

# Unit Test 5:

## *For Lessons 21-25*

Marks

/8 **1.** Review question: What are the four points of the SAT plan?

(1) ______________________

(2) ______________________

(3) ______________________

(4) ______________________

/2 **2.** Write a sensible statement to replace the following silly statement: "If I fail in school, it proves I am a total failure in life, and I should hate myself."

______________________

______________________

/2 **3.** True or False: I am the way I am; I can never change.

/6 **4.** There are four areas where some students at Hometown High were getting into trouble at school. The first is given here; list the other three areas.

(1) trying to get everyone's attention

(2) ______________________

(3) ______________________

(4) ______________________

/6 **5.** It is possible to disagree with adults in a fair, responsible way. List the three steps to do this:

(1) ______________________

(2) ______________________

(3) ______________________

/3 **6.** True or False: If you are fair with adults you will always get what you want from them.

/3 **7.** True or False: You should congratulate yourself for being fair, even if you do not get what you want.

/30 CRITERION TO PASS: 26

BONUS CHECKS: Report on two instances where you practiced the SAT plan.

# *Answers to Unit Test 5*

For guidance, see the "Getting Started" section of the introduction under Unit Tests. Each student should achieve at least the criterion indicated.

**1.** (1) Stop. Relax.

(2) Think sensibly.

(3) Make a plan.

(4) Congratulate.

**2.** Answers will vary here; here is a sample response: "Just because I fail in school, it doesn't mean I am a failure in life. I should always accept myself."

**3.** False

**4.** (2) Talking back to the teacher (showing I am the boss).
(3) Trying to make the teacher feel bad (getting even).
(4) Not trying (giving up).

**5.** (1) Ask for a time to have a talk.
(2) Politely state your concern. (Say how you honestly feel.)
(3) Thank the person.

**6.** False

**7.** True